CONTENTS

ACKNOWLEDGMENTS

First I want to thank my beautiful wife Kerri. You are my best friend and my inspiration!

To my mother Cheryl for showing me that having a positive attitude through any adversity is vital.

To my father Eric for instilling a good work ethic and compassion for others.

To my grandmother Marge for showing me that leadership by example and empowering others is the key to success in life.

To my mother-in-law LiChi for providing some of the best advice I've ever received in life.

To my father-in-law Robert for introducing me to the MLM profession.

To Michel Manuel for showing me that there is no adversity too big to stop someone from building a business.

To Nancy Dokter for helping me grow as a leader and for her willingness to learn from my lead.

To Pastor JB Kitts for being a loyal friend through the years.

To Ron Mattingly and Julie Riggs for going above and beyond what any company employee would ever do.

To Josh Henderson for daring to be different and having the belief in me to help him achieve his goals.

To industry trainers such as Eric Worre, Todd Falcone, Jordan Adler, Randy Gage, Jim Rohn, Zig Ziglar, Richard Brooke, Tom "Big Al" Schreiter, Robert Kiyosaki, Mark Yarnell, Art Jonak, and many more!

And to all of those whom I've had the pleasure to work with over my years in this incredible profession. Thank you for giving me the gift of leadership!

FOREWORD

If you've been involved in Multi-Level Marketing (MLM) (also known as Network Marketing) for any period of time then either you or someone you know has experienced what I'm about to share with you.

If you are new to this profession then the odds are good that you are on an incredible high. You've recently signed up with your company. You have your initial training complete. You most likely have attended your first live company event. It's safe to say that you are extremely excited about building your new business. On a scale of 1 to 10 with 10 being the most excited one could be you're probably at a 10.

So with your newfound excitement you begin to follow the company training. You make the contact list, pick up the phone and call your best friend, who you were just certain was going to join your business. You proceed to spend an hour on the phone with them explaining the intricate details of the company's compensation plan and the incredible benefits of using the life-changing product. And sure enough, the person you were certain was perfect for this, the person you were sure would be your first business partner, tells you that they aren't interested in being a part of your new business.

Your excitement level just dropped to a 4. So now you go for another phone call, because after all, your sponsor told you this was a numbers game. You pick up the phone and call your sister - whom you know without a doubt needs more money in her life more than anyone. You're thinking to yourself, "Surely my sister will get into this." You get your sister on the phone; spend an hour and a half explaining to her why she's crazy for not being a part of this "incredible opportunity." Does she join? No. In fact, the loving sister proceeds to tell you that you're in a scam and that you're going to go to jail if you stay in the business.

Your excitement level just dropped to a 1. This is the point where 95% of the quitters stop building their MLM business. It sounds ridiculous doesn't it? You've talked to two people and you're ready to give up on achieving your dreams.

If you've been a part of the MLM profession for more than a few months then the odds are good that either you've personally been through this or you have people on your team that are going through this right now. This book was designed to show you how to help yourself and others navigate the emotional roller coaster that is our wonderful profession of MLM.

I entered the MLM profession in 1997 at the age of 19. I was in college working towards a career in Physical Therapy. It took me 6 months to enroll my first distributor and he quit a week later. After 3 years of being a part of MLM (with the same company) I had put just 24 distributors on my team, and I think I paid for 23 of them to join. I was a rarity in that I stuck it out through those years with such poor results. The odds of someone sticking through the ups and downs of MLM are extremely small. My hope is that by reading this book you'll understand how I managed to survive this amazing ride so perhaps you too can achieve the lifestyle that you desire.

1 THE SECRET

Through all of my years in this profession I've discovered that there seems to be one common factor among all the top leaders in MLM - they didn't quit. They stayed with their company long enough and continued taking action consistently over that period of time in order to achieve the results they desired. Sounds easy enough doesn't it? The reality is that surviving the MLM emotional roller coaster is easier said than done. The foundation to it all (the secret) is that you need something that drives you internally. Something that makes you fight through the adversity and challenges you encounter. The "secret" is finding something that pushes you to build your business even when you don't want to.

The challenge is that most new MLM participants don't have a clue as to what that "something" is. Most of the time we're taught to define our "Why." We're told that we need to make a list of all the things we want in life: new cars, new home, new zip code, time freedom, etc. Now, don't get me wrong, you need to know where you're headed first. Of course that's vital. The hard part is that while these are all wonderful things that I certainly think we should be focusing on achieving, unfortunately for most people they aren't enough to push them to take consistent action.

I had the pleasure of going through Anthony Robbins' "*Personal Power II*" program. In that program Tony talks about what he feels are the two things that drive human behavior - pain and pleasure. I agree 100%. People in life are usually motivated by either pain or pleasure, or sometimes both. The same is true in our profession. Think about it for a minute - when you sit down to pick up the phone to start working your MLM business you are initially motivated because you want all the pleasurable things that being successful would give you. But what happens to most distributors? They don't make the calls do they? They avoid it like the plague. Have you ever heard that saying, "The phone can feel like it weighs 1,000 lbs.?" What is being described here is fear. Fear of being rejected, judged, ridiculed, etc. The fear of experiencing the pain that could be caused making that phone call is too much for people to handle so they just avoid doing it.

This is a classic case of the desire to avoid pain winning over the desire to achieve pleasure. It's actually pretty simple if you think about it. If pleasure were enough to motivate people then everyone would be successful because everyone desires pleasurable things. But it obviously isn't enough.

Why do most people get up and go to their J.O.B. each day? That's right, because they have to. If they didn't go they'd get fired. And then they wouldn't be able to feed their family, pay their bills, etc. The pain of potentially letting their family down is what forces most people to get up and go to a job that they can't stand. It's what pushes them to keep doing the same thing day in and day out for 40 to 50 years of their life.

To us as MLM professionals it sounds crazy for someone to go through that, but that's an illustration of how big of a motivator pain is in people's lives. It's the little part of our subconscious that we don't talk about in public. It's the part of us that tries to keep us safe and protected. And unfortunately this is something we're taught. From the time we're little we're taught to play it safe and take the path of least resistance. The good news is that this mindset can change. We can condition ourselves to use pain and pleasure to our advantage in our businesses.

Find Your Pain

For my first three years in Network Marketing/MLM I treated the business like a hobby. That's why I had very poor results. What I didn't realize at the time is that I didn't have anything driving me to build my business - I hadn't found my pain. And because of that it was too easy not to work my business. Sure, I had a vision board with fancy cars and a jet and a detailed description of my perfect day, but I still wasn't taking consistent action.

I remember thinking I was working my business consistently and hard but in reality I wasn't. It would be a Saturday and I'd wake up early and go to the weekly Saturday training at our local training center from 10 am until 2 pm. I'd come home, check the company voice broadcast tool (remember this was 1997) and listen to an hour's worth of training voice blasts that various leaders put out. Then I'd get on the Internet and surf around the different websites for our company. I'd create my 10th version of my super duper flyer (that I never put out by the way). Then I'd surf the web a little more, looking at some forums, chatting a little with people (offering advice to others when I'd never really done anything with the business). At the end of that day I'd think to myself, "Well I sure worked hard in my business today." Keep in mind I didn't dial a single contact, I didn't invite anyone to a presentation, didn't do any follow-up calls, didn't enroll a distributor or a customer.

Sound familiar? Unfortunately this is a typical "business day" for an average Network Marketer. Millions and millions of people all over the world filling their time with little extracurricular activities all in an effort to avoid taking action in their business. Why? Because they're afraid of experiencing the pain associated with actually doing the business. The key is turning the idea of avoiding pain around and using it as your motivating factor to build your business rather than avoid it.

> *"Fear is not real. It is the product of thoughts you create. Danger is very real, but fear is a choice."*
>
> *-Unknown Author*

I had been in MLM for three years and hadn't really done anything with it but then something happened. I found my pain and I didn't even know it at the time. My wife Kerri and I decided to start a family and it was really important to her that she be home to raise our kids. That may not seem like a big deal to some but it was huge to us and we weren't going to be able to do it on my income alone. Kerri was a Microbiologist and she was a good portion of our income. So I made a promise to her that I would replace her income. Making that promise to my wife gave me the motivation that I never had before. All it would take was one look at her and it was a constant reminder of the promise I made to her. It was the fear of experiencing the pain of letting her down that was my motivating factor.

I remember driving home from my job in Physical Therapy after working all day. I'd come in the house, I'd see the San Francisco Giants on TV and the last thing I wanted to do was head into my office and work my business. But there was Kerri. Tired from her long day at work too. I could see the desire she had to be at home and not away from her family. It killed me to see her. That was exactly what I needed! Even though I hated rejection. Even though I hated dealing with negative people. Even though it was hard to work more hours at home after I spent all day working at my J.O.B, seeing her reminded me of the promise I made. That was enough to push me to build my business, even when I didn't want to. That's all I needed to stay active in building my business, taking consistent action over a sustained period of time.

If you're new to this profession or if you're like I was and you've been floundering about in the profession, then I'd encourage you to certainly focus each day on what you want to achieve (pleasure) but to identify the pain that would be caused if you don't achieve it.

For example, perhaps your goal is to pay off your credit card debt so you can buy your family's first home. That's an incredible goal and it's something you should focus on achieving. But has that been enough to motivate you to consistently build your business to this point? If not then I'd suggest looking at it a little differently. Think about what will happen if you don't get rid of that debt. What will happen to your credit? What will that mean to your family's lifestyle? How will that affect their future? Look at the reality of you not achieving that pleasurable goal straight on and be honest with yourself. It's going to hurt your family if you don't get that debt paid off. Look at that pain and use it to motivate you!

Maybe you're part of a nutritional MLM company and your main product is a weight loss product, which is why you joined - because you want to lose weight. Everyone wants to lose weight because it would bring pleasure to do so. It would bring them pleasure to be attractive to others and feel good about themselves. But if that desire for that pleasure is enough why aren't you staying consistent with using your company's product to lose weight? The answer is simple, because it's easier not to follow the company program and to just eat the pleasurable foods you desire. So instead of focusing on wanting to be skinnier and look better, look at it a different way. Think about what's going to happen if you don't get the weight off. Do some research on early onset diabetes, cancer, and heart disease. Educate yourself about the life threatening dangers of obesity and use that as your motivation to follow the program.

I know, you think it sounds like I'm telling you to focus on the negative. But I'm actually not. I'm suggesting that you let your goals and your why be your destination (where you're headed) but let the fear of not achieving that (the fear of experiencing the pain of not reaching that goal) be the motivating factor that pushes you on a daily basis. That's the key, to consistently take that action each day over and over and over again - until you've reached your goal.

2 SELLING OUT

Now that you've laid a solid foundation it's time to start building your business. Before you do that you've got to have the right mindset. That starts with believing 100% in what you're doing. I call it "selling yourself out."

Having posture and a little bit of attitude is critical to getting positive results in our profession. It's vital when you're out recruiting new business partners and customers. Selling out completely is also a major factor in navigating the emotional ups and downs of building your business. If you don't believe in what you're doing and where you're going then nothing else matters. There are three key areas that you need to truly be sold out on. First you must be sold out on the MLM profession. Second is the opportunity you've chosen to be a part of. The Third area you have to sell completely out on is yourself.

Let's talk about all three...

The MLM Profession

I call it a profession because that's what it is. It's a profession that currently produces over $180 billion dollars worldwide (according to the Direct Selling Association). It's a profession that has many people earning seven figure incomes and many more earning six figure incomes. It's a profession that allows average people to achieve above average lifestyles - allowing the pleasure of experiencing both time and money together. It's a profession and you should be thinking of it as one.

Unfortunately most people think of MLM as "part-time" or a "hobby" type of business. This stems from the fact that there are so many people involved in the industry. This leads to a tremendous amount of people not doing very much which tends to have a negative impact on the public's perception of the MLM profession.

The best thing about MLM is also the worst thing. The best thing is that it's very inexpensive so anyone can get involved. This is great because in any economy there are many people that need a solution to their financial situation. Unfortunately the fact that it's so inexpensive to start a MLM business means that anyone can get involved. This leads to a lot of people "in" the profession but most of those people are not really working their business. This can lead some to think that the average person can't be successful in MLM and of course this weakens their belief in the profession.

Have you ever heard that saying from the MLM skeptics that "97% of the people in MLM fail?" Where do you think that comes from? My guess is it comes from the fact that there are so many people in MLM treating it like a hobby rather than a serious business that it leads to a lot of people doing very little or nothing at all. The reality though is that 97% don't fail. I would say that 97% don't earn a six-figure income, that is a proven statistical fact. But that's no different from any profession. I would bet 97%+ of Real Estate professionals don't make a six figure income either and that doesn't mean being a Real Estate agent isn't a good way to generate an income. The real truth is that 97% just aren't producing the effort to earn that type of income.

Top Global Sales for 2015

NFL...$12 BILLION
Music Industry...$15 BILLION
Movie Industry...$38 BILLION
Organic Food...$80 BILLION
Video Gaming...$91 BILLION

Direct Selling...
$183.7 BILLION

I'd also suggest that there are a great number of people in MLM that are reaching their goals every day. For instance, what if someone joins your company and their goal is to earn $500 per month in their business because they want to have a retirement fund. If they achieve that then they are a huge success in my mind. But the skeptics think that because they aren't earning a six-figure income then they've failed. That's not fair at all. You have to take into consideration the time and effort people are putting into their business. People often confuse time in the business with time actually building the business.

Let me explain it this way. Let's say that there are two pilots (call them Pilot A and Pilot B) who have both received their pilot's license and have both "been" pilots for 5 years. Pilot A has logged only 100 hours of flight time in those 5 years and pilot B has logged over 10,000 hours of flight time over the same period of time. Which one would you be more comfortable flying with? Which one is a more accomplished flyer? That's right, pilot B. They've both been pilots for the same number of years but one is obviously more successful than the other.

Compare that to Network Marketing. I was in my first MLM business for 3 years and had only 24 distributors on my team. There were other people who had been in the same company for 3 years or even less that had 24,000 on their team. We had both been "in the business" for 3 years but obviously we've had very different results. The fact of the matter is that I just hadn't logged as many flight hours.

One of the best discoveries I ever made was finding Tim Sales and his tool, The Pocket Tracker™ (www.firstclassmlmtools.com). This product completely changed my business. The tool basically helped you assign points to the daily activity that actually produced income in your business. You received points for things like making dials to qualified contacts, setting appointments, having guests attend a presentation, enrolling customers and distributors, etc. At the end of every day I would tally my points and put them into the monthly tracker, which would give you an idea of whether or not you were growing. Your goal was to have a high "daily point value" average for the month. What this did for me was show me that I wasn't being consistent in my business. I'd work hard for a week and then do nothing for the next three weeks. Or I'd work hard on Saturdays but do nothing throughout the rest of the week.

The problem with MLM is that too many people are running around with no focus and no method of operation. Creating something like Tim's tracker will help you stay on track and more importantly help you focus your time and energy where it really should be - working the business rather than surfing the web.

What I'm getting at is you can't hold the MLM profession accountable for the fact that most of its participants don't produce consistent action in their business. You can't say that it's a bad profession or industry because the majority of those involved don't get results with it.

I remember a conversation I had with my friend Tim who was a Personal Trainer at a gym. I had asked him to look at my business and his response to me was, "Oh, it's MLM, I could never do one of those things." I asked him why and he told me, "Because I couldn't sleep at night knowing that a large percentage of people signing up weren't going to be successful."

When he said that I just stood there and smiled. I proceeded to ask him, "Tim, how long have you been a Personal Trainer?" He replied, "15 years." Then I asked him, "In those 15 years about how many people have you trained?" He told me, "At least 1,000." To that I replied, "So out of the 1,000 people you've trained how many followed through with your program and reached their desired goal?" He sat there for a moment (I think he was starting to see what I was getting at) and he said, "Well, um, maybe about 50."

I looked at him with a bigger smile on my face this time and I said, "So you're telling me that 95% of the people who pay you money to train them don't succeed? How do you sleep at night?"

Tim wasn't smiling but the light bulb certainly had gone on. He knew what I was referring to. He knew that it wasn't his fault that his clients didn't succeed much the same way it isn't Network Marketing's fault that its participants don't either. At the end of the day it's up to the individual to take what they are taught and to see the job through.

Tim's perception is typical of people who don't understand our profession. To the ignorant out there, they feel that Network Marketers set out to take advantage of people when in reality it's the complete opposite. Professional Network Marketers seek out to empower and change the lives of people – just like Tim the Personal Trainer. Do we have some bad apples in our profession? Of course we do. But what industry doesn't? I believe there are far more scams and scandals in traditional business than there are in MLM. All you need to do is watch the evening news and you'll see an expose on the latest corporate scam that went all the way to the top.

You have to fall in love with the MLM profession and why shouldn't you? This is an incredible industry filled with millions of people using it to achieve their goals. Spend some time learning about the profession and educating yourself about its origins. Attend MLM generic seminars and network with other professionals in our industry. Not only will you grow professionally but also you'll gain a bigger respect for this profession. And that is so important. If you don't believe 100% in the MLM profession it's going to come across in your recruiting. You shouldn't be hiding the fact that you're a Network Marketer. You should be proud to talk about it. If you don't, making it big in this profession is going to be very difficult.

Your Chosen Opportunity

For those of you who have been in your company for less than 60 days you're probably saying, "But my company is perfect, I don't need to worry about not believing in my company or opportunity, we're the best." Well if that's what you say now, trust me, in about 60 more days your tune will change. For those of you who have been in your company 6 months or more you know exactly what I'm talking about.

Let me spare you the suspense, there is no perfect company. It doesn't matter how long the company has been around or how much money the company has or how great the product is, there will always be issues that cause you to question your current opportunity. But regardless of those issues you must always be completely sold out when it comes to your company, the product, and what you have to offer people.

You should have the mindset that when you offer people the chance to join your opportunity that you're giving them a gift. If you don't feel that way then it's going to be very hard for you to last in your business. You've got to sell out on all areas because once again, your passion and conviction (your posture) that you hold in your voice when you talk to people about your business comes from your belief in it. You can't love the company but hate the product. You can't love the product but not respect your company.

You have a choice - to either jump into another MLM company or to run with what you have. What determines which direction you go, really depends on you. First of all, you obviously must like your company's product. If you don't truly believe the product is going to help people then how on earth are you going to be excited about referring it to others? Second, you have to respect the corporate leadership and what they're doing. This is a hard one because most MLM corporate owners and staff are not seasoned Network Marketers. On the one hand that's good, you want a corporate staff that knows how to run a corporation, not necessarily build an MLM downline. But on the other hand you want a corporate staff that understands the profession because Networkers certainly are a different breed.

Comprising a little here and there will be necessary. If you're in a good company with solid leaders, that has a great product and a fair compensation plan, and there's other people making money in your opportunity - then you've got nothing to complain about. You have to work on getting over the little shortcomings to allow yourself to fall in love with your company. One of my long time mentors Sherman Henderson once said, "You're not in our company until our company is in you." I believe that 100%.

You don't need to be one of these walking billboards with your company logo plastered on your forehead and tattooed on your back, legs and arm. But you need to be sold out on the company and product. You need to support corporate events with passion. You need to educate yourself about your company and their products. You need to consistently plug into presentations and trainings to remind yourself of what you fell in love with when you initially joined.

The problem is that too many Network Marketers look to the company to give them the belief and enthusiasm to build their business and then if they don't feel they're getting what they need they quit and jump to another company hoping to find what they're looking for. When they don't find it there either they jump to yet another company. This is where the term "MLM Junkie" comes from.

I want to tell you a story about my friend Billy. He came to me a long time ago looking for an opportunity to improve his life. He was tired of being in construction and desired a better life and more security for his family. He chose to look into Network Marketing and eventually met me and joined with me in my business.

He did all the right things we want our new distributors to do. He plugged into our team's system. He followed my lead. He put people on 3-way calls and he became a very good distributor. Soon he became an up and coming leader with a few hundred people on his team. He was being recognized at company events and was repeatedly asked to share his story on stage and on team calls.

Unfortunately Billy fell victim to his newfound fame. He stopped focusing on his personal income producing activities and began to manage his one solid producing leg. Over time that team saw him throttle back on his building efforts and they too eventually began to do the same. It wasn't very long until Billy's momentum had completely stalled out.

It was about that time when I began to get some emails and phone calls with little complaints about this and that. It started small and then over time they became bigger and bigger complaints. Soon he began to cast his negativity to other people, looking for justification as to why he wasn't excited any longer.

Soon after that I saw a post on his Facebook page about a competing MLM company. I called him up to ask him what was up and he replied with, "Oh, I'm just helping my wife kick start her new business." Don't forget Billy was new to MLM. He didn't know that I had heard that many times before. This was typical from someone who thought it would be okay to join another company and begin to recruit the people out of their previous company – as long as it wasn't in their name. Unfortunately for Billy he was just lying to himself and soon his true colors were exposed. He had joined the other company.

We parted ways and I wished him well. He made an attempt to grab some of our team members – even people outside of his team. He was successful with a few but not too many others. Luckily for them, they had seen this behavior before. But for Billy, he wasn't prepared for what he was about to embark on.

Billy had left our company for a new opportunity. He was excited again with his new venture. He had his passion back! What was even better was he now had a bigger list (all the people from the previous company he left). So with his new excitement he set out to build. Within 6 months Billy had left that company too. His reason why: "The company couldn't deliver on what they promised."

When I heard this I was so sad. I truly wanted Billy to be successful in our profession but I had seen this pattern before. Billy had lost his focus on his why and was looking to the opportunity he was in to give him the motivation to build.

Sadly he eventually went on to a few other companies. As of right now he has been involved with MLM for 8 years and as far as I know he's been in at least 8 companies.

Billy's story is nothing new to our profession. Countless numbers of people jump from company to company each time moving farther away from achieving their goals and easing their pain.

If you can take a step back and look at your company and you can realize that no company is perfect and you really love your product then you need to let yourself commit to it 100%. Push your chips in and go all in. It's the only way you're going to make it to the top of your company. You can't build a long-term business in MLM if you're constantly starting over in new companies. Companies make mistakes, people come and go, but none of that has to affect you.

Over my career in MLM there were a lot of people like Billy in my team that quit along the way. I am so glad that I stuck it out because I've created a business that produces millions of dollars each year and the lifestyle that I always dreamed of. If I would have let adversity take me out of the game like those other people did then there's no way I would have achieved the level of success I have. Even more importantly, if I had given up I would have missed the opportunity to help the other people on my team achieve their goals.

Find a company and product you can believe in and then fall in love with it and sell out completely. You have a gift to offer people, something that can empower them to change their lives forever. Be excited about being able to give that gift to people!

Selling Out on Yourself

Being sold out on the MLM profession and the opportunity you're a part of is very important. Unfortunately it isn't the most important factor. Being sold out on you is the key. What I mean by this is you need to believe 100% in who you are, where you're going and that you deserve success in your life.

The reason this is so hard for beginners in our profession is they're most likely coming from a life of mediocrity. I don't say that to make you feel bad or to belittle them. I say it because it's a fact of life. 95% of our country is out there just getting by and people are being led to believe that playing it safe and following the path of least resistance is the best way to go. In other words, we aren't taught how to be and think like entrepreneurs.

Because we're not conditioned to have a success mindset we have to create one. This is why you see so many Network Marketers focusing on personal development. That's why you have this book in your hand. You realize that you need to grow as a leader and you're working at it.

Belief in you is what we're really talking about here. Believing that you can and will achieve all of your dreams. This will give you the posture and conviction you need to survive the MLM Roller Coaster. Solidifying this belief in yourself begins with finding your internal motivation. I mentioned this earlier when we discussed finding your pain. Knowing where you want to go and understanding the underlying factors that are pushing you to get there is vital. But you can't just think about where you want to be. You have to feel it. You have to be able to taste success even before you've had it.

Saying that and actually experiencing it are two very different things. So what can you do right now to experience success before you've had it? To start, you have to clearly understand where you're going and what you desire to achieve in your life. Earlier we discussed finding your pain. As you continue to ride the MLM Roller Coaster you'll see how important this really is. Once you have a strong hold on what's driving you then you're instantly given a crutch to lean on, and trust me you'll need many crutches. As negativity and adversity comes your way you'll be that much stronger because you believe in your mission 100%.

The next thing you can do is put yourself in environments and situations where you can actually feel success. When I finally decided to take my MLM business seriously I had created a vision board. On that vision board were things like my dream car, my dream home, my perfect day, pictures of my family, etc. And as much as I looked at that board there was always a little something in the back of my mind that wouldn't let me see it as a reality. So one day on whim I decided to stop by a local car dealership. There on the lot was my dream car. It was a $150,000 CLS 550 Mercedes Benz AMG and it was gorgeous. It was black with cream interior with black stitching. The steering wheel was wood and leather. It was an amazing car. I walked right up to the car salesman and said, "I want a test drive." He looked at me with a rather confused look. After all, I was a young 22-year-old kid wearing flip-flops, cargo shorts, and a t-shirt. But he agreed and off we went.

To this day I'll never forget how amazing that felt. The way the V8 engine roared, the 450 horsepower, the feel of the leather and wood in the steering wheel. It was powerful. We drove back to the lot, I handed the salesman the keys and simply walked off the lot in a daze with the biggest smile on my face. I drove home in my Toyota 4Runner still feeling the Mercedes steering wheel in my hands. That's all it took, I could now see myself worthy of being in that car.

A few months later I saw an open house for a multi-million dollar home in our city. I decided to go and check it out. I got dressed up and parked down the street (so the Real Estate Agent wouldn't kick me out of the house). She took me on a tour of an incredible home but when she took me into the home office I about fell over. It was amazing. I sat down at the desk into what was probably a $3,000 office chair and just sat there for about 15 minutes. That's all it took, I could see myself there.

From that day on I never doubted that I would achieve my goals, I felt them, they were real. And with my pain keeping me from procrastinating and slacking off I was now sold out on where I was going. Unfortunately this won't be enough for some people.

There are some that have extremely toxic lives. They might have family members that are highly negative or worse, their spouse may not support them in their business. It's very difficult to build a business when the people you love and are surrounded by each day are telling you to "give it up," and to "get back to reality." How are you supposed to achieve your goals with that being implanted into your subconscious each day?

Well the one thing I made sure I did was share with my loved ones why I was doing this. I started with my spouse. She needed to know that the reason we were going to be spending less time together temporarily was so that we would could have all the time we want in the future. I shared with some friends and family that there would be times when I couldn't go play golf or go to a ball game and I explained why. They didn't want to be in my business with me but at least now they understood why I was doing what I was.

Don't assume your loved ones can read your mind. Maybe to them they think you're just doing it to make some extra cash. Perhaps they have no idea your goal is financial freedom and security for you and your family. Have you tried sharing that with the people around you? If you haven't you should, immediately! You'll be amazed at how supportive people can be if you share your pain and your dreams with them.

Another thing I'd suggest that you do is surround yourself with positive influences. These can come in many forms. The first being personal development. Books, DVDs, CDs, magazines, etc. You should be spending at least 30 minutes per day listening or reading to something that helps you grow (remember this doesn't count as income producing activity). I'd also recommend surrounding yourself with like-minded people as much as possible. I know, you can't cut out all of your family and friends realistically but that's okay. Do your best to find some local leaders in your company. If you have a local training center or hotel meeting, make sure you're there each week. If you don't have one of those then find a networking program, there are many such as BNI, Toastmasters, and others. Network with professionals that are driven and positive and watch what rubs off on you.

And finally, find someone in your company that has the level of success you desire and plug yourself into him or her. Preferably this would be someone in your sponsorship line. They will have a financial benefit for helping you, which certainly helps their drive to help you succeed. Follow their lead and model their behavior.

When I was in my first company and I wanted to become a good leader I started mimicking the guy that was in our company's presentation video. He was a top leader in the company with more than 100,000 distributors on his team and he had made millions in our company. I actually transcribed his presentation word for word and memorized it. I would learn his jokes he used in the presentation. I copied the way he transitioned from section to section. Before I knew it I was sounding like him and sure enough my recruiting results improved - because I was improving.

Doing all of this helped me to raise my belief in me. But there was one piece of advice that I received at a company-training event that completely pushed my belief in myself over the edge. The leader was on stage talking about how beginners in MLM let the negativity of their family and friends effect their belief towards their businesses. He said something that I'll never forget. He said, "Don't you ever take the advice of people you don't want the lifestyle of."

That hit me like a lightning bolt. I immediately thought of family members who had ridiculed the MLM profession and my company and made me question my actions and myself. I reminded myself that these people were making less than $40,000 a year in a dead end job with no savings and no time freedom. Why would I listen to them? Then I had some family members who made $100,000 a year who did the same to me. And while at the time that was the kind of money I was looking to make, these family members were slaves to their jobs to make that kind of money. People working 60 to 70 hours a week and never seeing their family and always-stressed out on life. That wasn't what I wanted to be like.

Internalizing that advice helped me to keep my belief in myself and what I wanted to accomplish in life. My desire to avoid the pain of letting my wife down, coupled with my passion for Network Marketing and belief in myself is what drove me to push through to the other side. That's the point where massive daily action in your MLM business becomes a habit and actually a lot of fun. When you reach this point you no longer have to muster the motivation and drive to take action because it just happens. You become a machine because you are now "all in.

3 LAYING YOUR FOUNDATION

Now that you've found your internal motivation and you're completely sold out on yourself and where you're going, it's time to start building your business. But before you can do that you need to complete a few things first. I call it "laying your foundation." When you construct a building you start with the foundation first. This is the most important part because the rest of the structure relies on the foundation to be strong.

In our profession we call this "setting up our business." In your company you should have some sort of checklist or action plan that new distributors should follow to establish a good foundation to their business. If you don't have one then don't worry, just create your own, that's what I had to do. You can use some of the information in this chapter to help you but I'd encourage you to work with your leadership in your company to make sure that these steps apply properly to your system.

Maximize Your Potential

The first thing a new distributor needs to do is ensure they are qualified to get paid at the maximum income level in their compensation plan. Most MLM companies have different entry options when it comes to starter packages. They usually have a high-end option, a middle option and a low-end option. The high-end option is for the business builders - the people serious about creating a serious income. The middle option is for the people who aren't 100% sold out on MLM, their company or themselves. And the low-end option is for the people that just want to "try it out."

Personally I find it very hard to mentor someone who doesn't put themselves in the best position possible in their business. If someone comes to me and says "Ben, I want to be successful like you did, please tell me exactly what you've done and I'll follow your lead." My advice to them is then to start like I did - on the business builder package. If they say they don't want to do that then this is a huge red flag.

Now, I know there's going to be some people that just don't have the money to jump in at the higher package. That's completely understandable, especially in this economy. If that's the case for someone you're working with then they should be demonstrating a serious desire to build their business. They do this by being the person who brings the most guests to the presentations. They are the ones doing the most 3-way phone calls. They do their talking with their actions rather than their words.

Product of the Product

The next step is to become a walking testimonial for your company's product. In other words you're going to be a product of the product. How can you recommend a product to people when you aren't even using it yourself? Remember, one of the keys to being successful and surviving this amazing ride is being 100% sold out on the opportunity you're a part of. The product is the backbone to that opportunity so you must be excited about it. Better yet, you must have a story to share. If you look at all the top leaders in your company they all have an amazing story.

If you're in a product based business this is incredibly important since you're talking to people about a product they don't already have or use and you know they should be. Being able to tell your story is a great building tool. For example, I knew a gentleman in a nutritional company whose main product was a weight loss program. He lost 50 pounds in 90 days. He was a walking testimonial. I knew another person in a company that had an energy drink as their product. He would go around telling his story about how he's kicked coffee and soda and how great he feels. Another person was in a service-based company and he would talk about how he's saving thousands of dollars per year on his cell phone bill.

Whatever the case may be, you have to be on the product and passionate about what that product is going to do for people. If you don't feel this way about your company's product then I suggest you either do a little more research about the product and why it's so great or perhaps look for a different product and company to represent.

Plug Into the System

This is a business and it requires tools and a system to build it. Most companies supply their distributors with very poor systems and tools. If that's the case, I would recommend that you look to your leadership support team for the tools and systems that they suggest.

First you're going to need some basic business management tools. You should have some sort of contact management tool. There are many programs out there that can work fine. Even basic ones that come with your Outlook or Gmail accounts are adequate. For those of you that really want to take your business to another level I'd recommend creating your own email auto-responder database with a company such as Aweber or Constant Contact. Having the ability to blast out an email to your entire database of people you meet over the next few years will be a very valuable asset!

Next I would suggest setting up a business checking account. Credit Unions are very easy to work with and often have great incentives for businesses like interest bearing accounts or free checking accounts. If you're a beginner it may seem unnecessary to do this right now but trust me, it's going to make your life a lot easier as you build your business. It's really important to be investing the money you're making back into your business for your personal and professional development. I often see people who lump all their business money with their personal money forgetting about this and they end up paying for personal things with the money they make from their business.

Now, you might say, "But Ben, I thought MLM was all about making money to do what you want with?" And you're right, but we need you to get to the point where you have your business established first. There's too much work to be done in your business and on yourself to not be putting money back into it. Try to stay disciplined with this concept it will help you accelerate your growth dramatically. Remember, I'm here to help give you the insight into how I made it through the tough years of building a business in MLM. I'm only here to help!

The next step is to plug into your company and/or team training system. You should log into your company back office and get familiar with where to find answers to questions, where your commission and downline reports are, how to enroll distributors, customers, etc. Also get oriented with your different websites. Most companies supply their distributors with retail and marketing websites for customer gathering and for showing the opportunity to potential distributors.

Now would be a great time to set up a few domain names that are short and simple that you can put on your business cards, on your email signatures, etc. Set up domain name forwarding to point to the different websites. It's much better to have a domain name like www.joinxyz.com instead of http://yoursitename.yourcompanyname.com. It just looks more professional and it's a lot easier to give a short domain name over the phone.

Ordering your marketing tools is an important next step. Your team or company will likely have a system they're utilizing and I would recommend following their lead. Don't try to recreate anything here. If there are people in your upline leadership team that are getting results then follow their lead and keep it simple. As a new distributor there are some basic tools that will help you get much better results. Some sort of 3rd party DVD or sorting website is very helpful. This will be a way for you to sort through your contacts without wasting too much time with the wrong people (we'll get into that later on). You need a tool that you can either hand to someone in person or send them somewhere over the phone to a website where they can go and get exposed to your opportunity - without you having to physically be there or having to explain anything.

Remember, the moment you get on the phone with the people you're talking to, you're teaching them that what you're doing is exactly what they will have to do to build a successful business. If that seems too difficult then they won't be receptive to the opportunity. Let the system do the work for you.

Having some nice opportunity or product brochures is great as well. These can be used as a first look tool or as a follow-up tool. Our team uses this more as a follow-up tool, just another way to keep our prospective business partners plugged into our information. It also shows your contact that they'll have tools available to them so they don't have to be an expert.

> *"A good system shortens the road to the goal."*
>
> *-Orison Swett Marden*

The next step in setting up your business is to identify the schedule of events that your team and company are following throughout the weeks, months, and year. Most companies and teams have daily events to plug into such as webinars, conference calls, hotel meetings, super Saturdays, etc. You should be scheduling these events into your calendar and making it a priority to attend them. It's very important for you to surround yourself with the language of your company. The sooner you can get the "lingo" down the easier it will be for you to talk to people about your opportunity and the more effective you'll be at building your team.

Plugging into the next major company/team event is also a top priority for a beginner. At this point in their business they've walked up the stairs to the roller coaster and they're turn in line is almost up. They'll be stepping into the ride and getting strapped in very soon. A live major event as soon as possible will have a very important impact on the retention of this new distributor. I remember the first major event I went to with my first MLM company. There were over 40,000 people in an arena. Do you think that had a lasting impression on me? You bet it did. That kind of social confirmation is critical for new distributors. Even if the event only has 150 people in it, it's still critical.

The daily webinars and conference calls recruit the team but the major events build and bind that team together. Passion and conviction is contagious but you can't catch it on a conference call. Being surrounded by hundreds or thousands of like-minded people and being trained by the top people in the company has a very important impact on new distributors. The relationships that are created at these major events are also very important. If you don't have a team to bring with you to these events then you plug into your leadership and do your best to hang out with them. Find them in the lounge at the hotel. Try to tag along as they go to lunch (Tip: Don't let your upline pay for you - you offer to pay for them - it's classy move that will set you apart from everyone else that feels the upline should always get the check because they're making the big money).

I see it every year in my company. The people that attend the major national events are the ones that last longer and grow more successful businesses. As you continue on this roller coaster it's important to plug into three to four major national events per year. Yes, I know they can be expensive with the travel costs. But the money you're making from your business should be going directly into your business checking account and you should be budgeting for these events. If you haven't made any money yet then you're going to have to look at it as a financial investment.

You might be thinking to yourself, "I don't need the hype and rah-rah of these meetings, I'm excited enough and I'll do it on my own." If that's what you're thinking then you are in for a serious battle ahead. No matter how excited you think you are. No matter how good you think you are, building this business requires those crutches that I mentioned earlier. The major events will provide the biggest support to your MLM career than anything else. If you do nothing else in your first year in MLM you should attend every major national event your company has. It truly will change your life.

4 LAUNCHING YOUR BUSINESS

Now that you've laid down a strong foundation for your business it's time to start building it. You're on the roller coaster now. It's just beginning to start moving and begin the initial climb. You're nervous and excited at the same time. The adrenaline is pumping and now is the most critical time of your business.

When working with a new distributor I call this stage "launching their business." I call it that because my goal is to get them started fast, like a space shuttle launch. And like a space shuttle launch there are some key steps that need to take place in order for it to be effective. If there is no successful launch having an effective flight is almost impossible. My goal is to get them taking action in their first 24 to 48 hours. Our team has a system called the "Fast Start Launch System." (If you'd like a copy of what we provide our team you're welcome to contact me and ask for it). The first couple of days of a new distributor's business are the most critical time for them. You'll increase their odds of surviving the roller coaster significantly if you can get them taking immediate action in their business.

Build Your Contact Database

Making it through the emotional roller coaster of MLM requires that you are consistently showing new people your opportunity. To make that happen you have to build a large contact database - aka "your contact list." Having a big list will have a tremendous impact on your posture. If you have 500 people to talk to over the next 90 days then you're not going to care if 10 people tell you they aren't interested. However, if you have a list of 15 people and 10 tell you "no" then you've pretty much forced yourself to think that this business isn't for you.

So how do you create a large database of contacts? The first place to start is with what is commonly known as your "warm market." If you've been MLM before you're probably rolling your eyes right now. But before you skip this section I want to point out that not all the people you know extremely well (friends and family) are right for this profession. That's right, I said it, there are some people that shouldn't come within 100 feet of a Network Marketing company. The challenge is that you don't know who those people are. That's why you have to share this business with everyone! Notice that I said "share," not "sell."

This is where most beginners in MLM fail miserably. They create a list of perfectly good people and then they attempt to sell their opportunity to them. They use strange scripts and sales tactics to attempt to lure people into their opportunity. Not only does this not work but it's what gives our profession a bad reputation and leads to the massive amount of attrition our industry has. I'm going to teach you how to professionally and effectively work your warm market and I'm also going to show you how to constantly be adding new names to that contact database.

Why the Warm Market

When I help launch a new distributor and we work to create their initial list I always suggest they begin with their warm market. The problem is most beginners proceed to make a list of their friends and family members **only**. That can be a problem if most of their friends and family are broke minded, skeptical and negative. If they are driven, money motivated, people-people then it can be a great place to start. The challenge is that you really can't pre-judge whether or not someone is right for the opportunity or not - so you have to share it with everyone. We'll get into how to do that in a moment but first I want to explain why it makes so much sense to start with the warm market first.

The key to being a good recruiter is getting the people you're talking with to trust and respect you. If you attempt to begin your MLM career by talking to people you do not know then you must first have the skills to be able to get people to trust and respect you. When you are running advertisements or using any other method to generate leads for your business, the people responding to those ads are going to be looking for a leader to be able to guide, coach and mentor them. Someone that is new to the MLM profession obviously doesn't possess the skills and posture in order to illustrate that posture to their contacts, yet.

Recruiting in the cold market is more about how you sound on the phone than what you say. The passion and conviction in your voice is what leads people you do not know to lower their guard and begin to trust you. That opens the door to a potential working relationship. Someone new to the MLM profession certainly doesn't have that type of passion in his or her voice. Why? Simple, because they're brand new. They may be excited about their opportunity but they haven't been successful in MLM yet so of course they aren't as confident as someone who has.

Taking a beginner in MLM and immediately putting them into the cold market is setting them up for immediate failure. Similarly, sending them out into their warm market to go after the wrong people can also be setting them up for failure.

So how do you know who is right and who isn't? Unfortunately there's no real easy answer to this question. I always encourage people not to pre-judge whether or not someone is right for the opportunity because there are countless stories of people from all different backgrounds and socioeconomic situations that had success in our profession. But I think we can all agree that successful leaders in the MLM profession do have some underlying characteristics. Most are driven, money motivated, and have large circles of influence. Therefore, targeting those types of people will help you to accelerate your success in your business.

These are the people that we "go after." These are the people that we approach directly with an offer to have them look at our amazing business opportunity - because we feel they would be a valuable asset to our team. Think of yourself as a talent scout. You're looking for talented people that you see as an asset.

> *"When you judge another you don't define them, you define yourself."*
>
> *-Wayne Dyer*

Now, what about the people on the warm market list that doesn't fit that description? You know the types I'm talking about. The grumpy aunts and uncles. The lazy cousins. The "never think outside the box" brother-in-law. Do we simply leave them out? No, of course not. With these people, we're going to plant the seed, but we're going to do it in a way that doesn't leave you with friends and family avoiding you.

In our business we approach these people with an offer to benefit from our product. The approach will vary from company to company depending on the product but in general the idea is the same. Instead of picking up the phone and calling your grumpy uncle and saying, "Uncle Joe, do you keep your options open to new business ideas," you might shoot uncle Joe an text or a quick phone call that says, "Uncle Joe, I've recently started a business and we have a great product that helps people _____ (insert the benefit of your product). If you know anyone looking for that type of benefit I would greatly appreciate the referrals. Here's my website and business line..."

If you look at that approach you see that you're not opening up an opportunity to get shot down. You aren't putting grumpy uncle Joe in a situation where he's going to try and "school" you on the realities of business (after all, he's an expert in business - even though he's never made more than $40,000 a year in his life). This approach can be done with every single person you know that you don't feel is an ideal candidate for your business. At the very least you're planting a seed in the minds of those people. That way, should grumpy uncle Joe ever have a need for your product or perhaps has a desire to create additional income, he'll know what you're involved in and he may just come to you.

There are literally millions of stories in our profession of people who had family and friends join their company under someone other than them. There are millions more of family and friends joining other competing companies as well. This happens because people aren't planting the seed with everyone they know. I can't tell you how critical it is to take the advice of your leadership and truly make a contact database of every single person you have any connection with.

The key is to think outside your close circle. When I ask someone I'm working with to begin making their list of 100 contacts they usually say, "But Ben, I don't know 100 people." Of course they do. The average 20 year old knows the first name of over 1,000 people. They just aren't thinking of them at that moment.

The initial list you make the day you join will be your closest friends, family and acquaintances. But you must expand that list. One way to do that is by using your existing databases. With social media these might be your contacts on Facebook. Your cell phone has a contact database. Your email has a contact database.

Another method I've found effective is using the yellow pages. Start with "A" for Accountants, Attorneys, Auto Repair, etc. Write down all of the people that you know of in those professions. Even if you don't know these people on a personal (friend) basis, write them down. Even if it's a place you do business. Repeat this process going A through Z and watch how many names you come up with.

Another great thing to do is thinking about your profession or your passions and look to network with people who share those same interests. For example, if you're a teacher then that pretty much makes every teacher in the world part of your warm market! Think about it: you share a common profession. A simple phone call or email to someone saying, "I'm a former/current teacher as well and I wanted to connect with you…" could yield a new person on your list.

Perhaps you're interested in knitting. Get on the knitting message boards and connect with people. No, I'm not saying go on the boards and blast your ad for your product or opportunity. I'm saying get on there, contribute to the message board and make some new connections. Instant warm market!

People that you know of or associate with are also included in your "warm market list." The fact that you have some sort of connection to them - even if it's through a 3rd party - means that you have an instant "in" with them. This is critical because it almost immediately gives you the trust you're looking to gain in prospecting.

Starting with the warm market allows you to be who you are - someone who is excited about your new venture but someone who hasn't been successful yet. With your warm market you don't have to be the expert with posture. All you need is to be excited about getting them the information. To be effective at getting people to the information it's vital that you follow a system that is simple and effective at getting people the information they need to make an educated decision on whether or not your opportunity is right for them.

5 A SIMPLE SYSTEM

At this point you have begun to build your database. You're now going to start reaching out to those people. To do this effectively and help insure your survival of the MLM Roller Coaster, you must have a simple and proven system to plug people into. If you're working in a company that has been around for at least one year then there's most likely a system in place that is getting results for the top leaders of your company. My recommendation is to find out exactly what that is and follow what their system suggests. It should look something like the following...

Step 1: Pique Interest/Invitation
Step 2: Show The Plan
Step 3: Follow-up/Validation
Step 4: Enroll/New Team Member Launch

The components of this system are different from company to company but in general the guidelines are basically the same.

Step 1: Pique Interest

This is the step where you are picking up the phone to invite your contact to look at your company's presentation. This is the most critical step of all because if you mess this step up nothing else can take place. This is why fear begins to set in. You realize that everything is riding on this phone call and this is where call reluctance sets in. To overcome that fear you have to fall back on your pain. Remember - it's that "something" in you that's pushing you to do this - even when you'd rather not!

The first step needs to be very simple. One thing I was taught by my mentors in this profession is that the moment we say hello to our contacts, we're teaching them exactly what they're going to have to do to be successful in our business. If you keep that in mind you should remember to keep this process simple.

What you need to understand is what your goal is. At this point your goal is not to enroll a distributor. Your goal is not to earn a check. Your goal is not to gain a promotion or to even build a residual income. At this point of the process your goal is to simply find out whether or not this person is interested in learning more about your opportunity. The more you say during this process the less likely your prospect will be interested in learning more.

This is a very hard concept for beginners to understand. I remember when I was brand new. I went home from my first hotel opportunity meeting and joined on the spot. I put $700 on a credit card (that I had no way of paying back) took my sponsor's kit home with me (he had been in a day longer than I had), read the entire kit and stayed up until 2 am memorizing the information. The next morning I picked up the phone and called the first person on my list, my best friend Dylan - a person I was just certain would join my business with me. I spent the next hour and forty-five minutes regurgitating everything I'd read the night before in the kit. My excitement and enthusiasm had gotten the best of me. I was now taking Dylan into what I call "The Valley of Death."

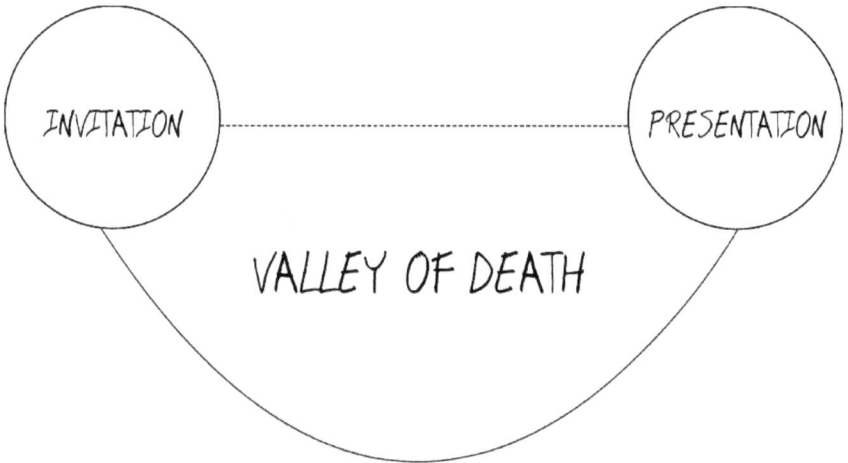

This is where our contacts go and they do not return. It's the space between our pique interest call and the presentation. It's where we try to explain why we're so excited about our opportunity and instead of keeping it simple and passing their interest on to a simple system we blab and blab and blab about percentages, levels, bonuses, product features, how regular jobs are pyramids, etc. To sum it up in a few simple words: we confuse the heck out of our contacts.

Do you think Dylan joined with me? Of course he didn't. In fact, my best friend avoided me for two weeks! This was the first person on my list, the person I was certain would do this and he didn't. My excitement level shot straight down from a 10 to a 4!

So what did I do wrong? Well, for starters I said too much. I scared Dylan off because I made him think that to be a part of my business he was going to have to memorize a bunch of facts and numbers. The second mistake I made was by not following a simple system to pique his interest, and then pass that interest on to the presentation.

Many companies offer some incredible tools to help you with this step. I call these tools "bridge tools" to help you bridge the gap between the pique interest step and presentation.

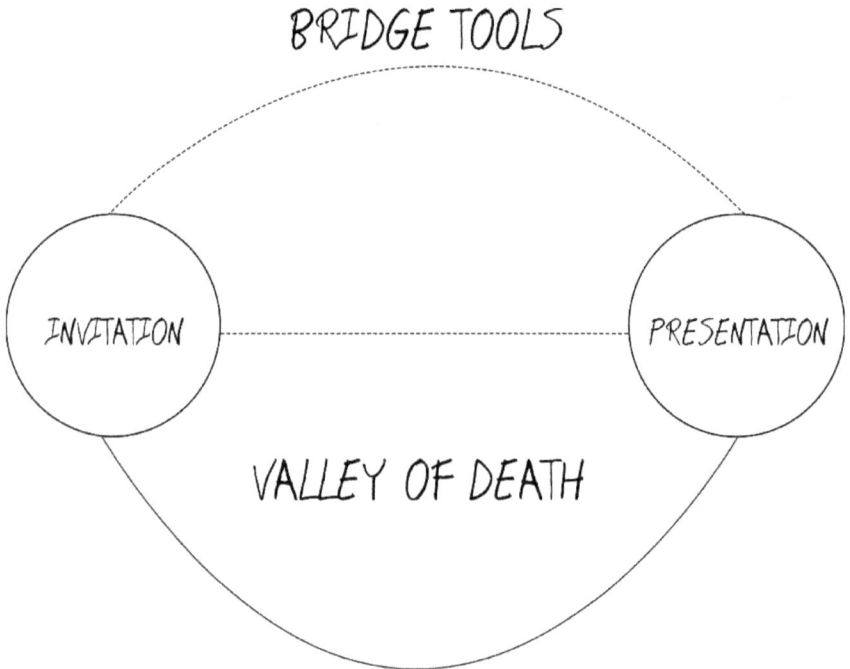

BRIDGE TOOLS

INVITATION — — — — — — — — — — — PRESENTATION

VALLEY OF DEATH

It might be a bridge message (a short 2 or 3 minute recorded phone message about your opportunity done by a top leader in your company that piques the interest of your contact for you). It could be a nice company brochure/magazine, a DVD, a website, etc. It can also be just you that piques your contacts interest. If you feel confident in your abilities to pick up the phone and call the talented people in your database then go for it! You might say something to the effect of, "Hey Dylan, if I could show you a way to create some additional income without taking anything away from your current job, would you be willing to look at something on the web for me?"

The danger zone comes when Dylan says, "Well sure Ben but what is it?" If you start to answer that question like I did years ago then that's when you're holding your prospects hand as you lead him into the Valley of Death! To avoid this simply pique the interest and pass the interest on to the presentation and system. What I should have said to Dylan years ago (but didn't of course) was, "Well Dylan, this website is going to show exactly what this is all about. I don't know if it's for you or not but I would really appreciate you taking a quick look at this for me and judging for yourself."

Notice how we aren't pushing an opportunity down someone's throat. I'm not tricking Dylan into having coffee with me and then hitting him with an opportunity presentation. I'm not inviting him over to a "barbeque" and then making him sit through a Private Business Reception done by my team leader. What I'm doing is called sorting. I'm letting Dylan look and judge for himself. I'm letting Dylan see how simple the system is and I'm not wasting time with someone that may not be right for my business.

Now, this may go against what some people teach in this profession. In fact I know it does. There are some leaders that teach you to sit down with everyone you know, get them to a one on one or home meeting and talk until you're blue in the face and convince everyone you know to join with you and basically tell the people who don't join with you that they're crazy and are going to be broke for the rest of their lives. I am not from that school of thought. The way I feel is that it's a lot more fun to build a business where a) I work with people that want to be a part of my business because of their own reasons not because I talked them into it and b) a business that has a system where people will feel comfortable and excited about sharing it with others.

Remember the goal of step 1 is to pique interest. All we're trying to do is get them to the next step where they can see the big picture - the presentation. In other words our only goal is to get them to the exposure process. We're going to expose our business to them and then let them make the decision to join from there.

Step 2: Show The Plan

Just as there are many tools for piquing interest there are many tools to show your company's business overview. Whatever method you decide to use it must be something other than you. Any 3rd party tool that highlights your company's product and opportunity works just fine. The more effective methods for presenting are live events. It could be a live web presentation, hotel presentation, home meeting, or even a conference call.

The reason you shouldn't be the one doing the presenting is for the social validation. If you have used an effective tool to introduce your contact to your opportunity then they most likely have a pretty good idea of what it's about and whether or not they're interested in being a part of it. What they need now is validation that this is bigger than just you. This is especially important if you're talking to someone that you know. The people you know most likely are aware of the fact that you don't know much about your company's product. Unless you have a background in the field associated with the product then it's likely you don't have a lot of credibility with your warm market.

That's where the live events come in. They act as the validation to show your contacts that 1) this is bigger than just you and 2) that there is a system in place to do the presenting for them. This is critical because again, this entire team your contacts are asking themselves, "Can I see myself doing this?" If they can't they won't join, it's as simple as that.

My favorite way to show a presentation is a live event. Webinars and group meetings are best because they accomplish two very important things. First, they create the social validation that you're looking for. The second thing they do is allow you to be more efficient in your exposures. It's my opinion that the days of the "one-on-one" presentation are over. I feel this way because it's very difficult to duplicate. The average person is a lot busier today than they were 15 years ago. Most people don't have the extra time to show 4 or 5 presentations at Starbucks in a day. Yes, a top producer can easily do that, but then where do you get your duplication?

It's my opinion that duplication comes by plugging people into a system that everyone can use over and over again and it maximizes the time they have to invest in their business. For this reason I really love the live webinar. Our team does live webinars throughout the week, every week. We do this because it allows all of our team to spend their day on the phone with prospects while piquing interest and at the same time giving them a live event to push people into for another exposure.

The webinars are a lot easier to duplicate in your organization because no one has to book a room in a hotel, set it up, put on the show, etc. In other words, webinars are fairly turn-key. Now, that does not mean I don't think you shouldn't have or plug into live hotel events, you certainly should. I prefer them more in a training format - such as a once per week Saturday training, or maybe once per month. Live hotel events are critical to bind the team together. It's where you create the synergy and momentum and they are critical to success. But let's face it, the name of the game in the MLM profession is getting your business in front of as many prospects as you can. If that's the case does it really make sense to only do one live hotel presentation per week? Wouldn't you want the opportunity to show people your business every day?

If your leadership team isn't currently using a live webinar system that's okay, continue to use the system they are training on, but you might also consider adding your own webinar presentation for your own personal team to plug into. There's nothing wrong with you finding more ways to be more effective and efficient in presenting your business to people.

One aspect of the webinars that I like is they make it a little easier to get prospects to actually show up. Have you ever heard your upline say something like, "If you want 1 person to show up at the hotel meeting then invite 10 people?" Well, webinars can help improve your guest attendance greatly, simply because they're easier to attend. Your prospect doesn't have to drive anywhere, get dressed up or put the kids with a sitter. They also like the fact that they won't be in a room filled with hyped up Networkers pressuring them to join.

Creating urgency for your prospects to attend the presentation is a great way to also increase attendance. This is true whether you're using a live hotel meeting or a live webinar to present your opportunity. The urgency and excitement they hear in your voice is a big reason why they'll attend. Passion and excitement is something that everyone wants and the more you can exude that in your tone and how you sound on the phone the more effective you'll be at getting guests to attend your live presentations.

Something else you can do to help increase guest attendance is to do what I call a "double confirmation." About an hour or two before the presentation is to begin, give your guests a quick phone call and say something to the effect of, "Hey Joe Prospect, I just wanted to give you a quick call and make sure you had the right website for tonight's live web presentation. It's really important to me that you attend and I don't want you to miss out on what we're going to cover."

Then of course you need to attend the live event as well. It sends a terrible message to your guests if you invite them to the webinar and you don't show up yourself. It also sends a bad message to your team. After all, if you're not there why should they be? Now, you might be saying, "But Ben, I've heard the presentation 1,000 times, do I really need to sit and listen to it every night?" Of course not! If you've heard the presentation enough and you're able to recite it word for word then of course you don't need to sit through it. What I would do is log myself into the web room so my team and my guests see me there and then I'd get on the phone and make more calls and start inviting people to look at the presentation for the next night.

Step 3: The Follow-up

Yes, the cliché is true, the fortune is in the follow-up. A quick and direct follow-up is critical to success in MLM. Too many Network

Marketers leave open ended invitations and they wonder why their contacts never actually go and look at the information they've asked them to. That means an effective follow-up actually begins in the initial piquing interest stage.

When you invite someone to look at your company's information playing it cool won't work. You can't say, "Oh it's no big deal, take a look when you get a chance and we'll get back together in a few days." Or, "Take a look at it and I'll give you a call in the next day or two." Or worse, "Take a look and let me know if you'd like to get started."

> *"Diligent follow-up and follow-through will set you apart from the crowd and communicate excellence."*
>
> *-John C. Maxwell*

As I mentioned earlier the urgency in your voice is critical. After all, if you aren't excited about your opportunity then why should your contacts be? The problem in this day and age of MLM is that some people feel that being excited is somehow associated with being too aggressive or "pushy" for your prospects. While there can be some extremely overbearing Network Marketers, most people handle their invitations with respect for their contacts.

You don't need to fill people with cliché's about "getting rich with no effort" or "making money while we sleep" in order to create urgency. It's simply the tone in your voice when you say something as simple as, "Joe, I don't know if this is for you but you have to take a look at this. What are you doing tonight at 7 pm? There's a live web presentation you've got to see."

Now, once they agree to take a look this is the time to begin an effective follow-up. "So Joe, the presentation is at 7 and it will last for about 30 minutes. It's vital to me that you take a look at this. Can I count on you attending tonight?" After he agrees, "Wonderful Joe. Listen, it would be great if we could talk right after you've looked at this information, are you going to be free at 7:45 after the presentation for a quick follow-up call?" If he is then book the follow-up. If he isn't then book it for as close to the time when he looks at the presentation as possible. You want to get on the phone with your contacts while they have the information fresh in their mind so you can help them make an educated decision on whether or not your opportunity is right for them.

When you conduct that follow-up call you need to be prepared. The first thing you need to be prepared for is the idea that this person may not be as excited as you are about joining your business. One of the most challenging things new distributors go through is the misguided expectation that everyone will join their opportunity or see the brilliance of their opportunity like they did. You might be saying, "Oh Ben, I know it's a numbers game and that it's not for everyone." But in reality in your subconscious you're thinking to yourself, "Everyone has to join my business because it just makes so much sense and they'd be crazy not to want to be a part of it."

Remember my conversation I shared with you about my friend Dylan? Do you remember how crushed I was when he didn't join? My excitement level dropped from a 10 to a 4 with my first conversation. The reason was because I was like most people and truly couldn't believe that Dylan didn't see what I saw in that business. What I know now is that the reason people don't join your opportunity has nothing to do with you, your upline, your product, your presentation, etc. It has everything to do with the timing in their lives. If the timing in their life is not right for an opportunity then nothing you do or say is going to change that. Realizing this takes the pressure off and you can get excited about simply exposing your business to as many people as you can in an effort to find the people for whom it is right for.

Next, you need to be prepared for the questions your contacts are going to have. In most cases people aren't going to attend your presentation and then be ready to join. That may happen once in a while but for most people they're going to need some questions answered before they decide to join. Now, if you're new to your business then you aren't expected to be able to answer the questions. But I'd recommend never saying the words "I don't know." It doesn't instill a lot of confidence in your contacts if you come out and say to them that you really don't know what's going on. So if someone asks you a question that you don't know the answer to I'd recommend you say, "You know Joe, that's a great question and I'm going to get all of your questions answered but before we get into that I'd love it if you took a little time and..."

You can fill the next sentence with many things. What we're talking about here are additional exposures. Typically prospects need 3 to 5 exposures before they make a decision to join. So this is a great opportunity for you to get them exposed to more information while at the same time buying some time while you find the answer to their question or perhaps scheduling a 3-way call with your upline support team.

You might expose them to your product page at this point or your opportunity website for your company. Any additional 3rd party tools can help add more exposures. And once again, it further validates that there will be tools and systems in place for your prospect so they don't have to memorize a bunch of information.

Now, I do have to say that being knowledgeable about your company, product, compensation plan, etc. does help. There is nothing wrong with having a longer conversation with your contact at this stage of the process. Your contact has been exposed to the presentation so they've seen the big picture and they have a foundation to base your conversation on. This follow-up conversation is a great opportunity for you to share your story and tell your contact what you love about this opportunity. It's also a great time to edify your upline and system that you're a part of. People love to be a part of a winning team and you should use that to your advantage. Talk about the support you're receiving. Talk about the leaders that are a part of your leadership team supporting you.

Finally you need to be prepared to be able to know the difference between objections and questions. Sometimes people just don't want to be a part of your business but they don't know how to just say, "no." Instead they throw objection after objection at you and you spend hours coming back with a response to every objection they have. You shouldn't be wasting your time answering objections, you should be spending your time answering questions.

So how do you know what's an objection and what's a question? Well, it comes down to you learning how to read people's tone as well as the words that come out of their mouths. For example, if someone says to me, "Well I don't have a lot of money is this going to cost me a lot?" That's an objection. If someone says to me, "Well you know Ben, things have been really tough for me this year and money is tight, but I really see this opportunity. Is there a way for me to be successful without spending a lot of money?" Do you see the difference in the tone and language of the question?

Another example might be, "Well I'm already working 50 hours a week, I don't have the time." Versus, "Well I'm already working 50 hours a week but I do want to change that. Do you have a system that allows someone to do this part-time?" Again, can you see the difference here? One is basically saying "No, I really don't want to do this," while the other is saying, "Yes, I really see it but I have some questions."

To become effective in the follow-up it's crucial that you get better at reading people. Spend most of your time in your follow-up listening to people to hear what they like about your opportunity. Then share your story about why you're excited. Bring your upline in to help if needed but as quickly as you can become the upline that has the answers. 3-way calls to the upline are very effective but if you want your business to grow quickly you can't rely on them as the main way you close your prospects. If it is then you're going to constantly be at the mercy of your upline's time and availability.

That leads me to the final aspect of the follow-up - "the close." I'm not the type of person that likes to use sneaky tactics to get people to make a buying decision. I'd rather share my opportunity with people, let them look and judge for themselves and then collect a decision. But I do understand that collecting that decision can be uncomfortable at times. So over the years I found a method that works very well for me.

After I've answered my contact's questions I can usually tell how interested they are. Sometimes people will ask directly for my website to go and join. But most of the time they do not. So after I feel they have the information they need to make a decision I ask a very simple question: "So Joe, if you feel like you're ready to get started the next step is to get you enrolled and schedule a launching session. In that session I'll take you through a tour of your back office, the training site and we'll work out a little game plan to get your business launched properly. Does that sound like something you want to do or do you need more information?"

If they baulk at this or there's any hesitation in their voice I know that they aren't serious about working with me. At that point I ask them if they need any more information, then I'll pass that on to them and tell them that when they're ready to get started to let me know. I will then put them in my contact database and I'll set a reminder to follow-up with them in the next 30 days.

That's really it. The follow-up doesn't have to be a complicated process. All you're doing is answering your prospects questions and helping them make an educated decision. Just remember that it's a lot more fun to work with people that want to be a part of your opportunity because of what they see rather than what you want them to see. Get excited about going through numbers and don't get bogged down spending too much time trying to respond to all the objections that are thrown at you.

Step 4: Enroll/New Team Member Launch

When most new distributors enroll a new team member they often think their job is done when in reality it's just beginning. Signing up a new team member is the easy part. The hard part comes in helping to launch that new team members business.

I'm sure that your team or company has some sort of system of training that they've put together for new distributors. But that alone isn't enough to get your new team members launched properly. I call it a launch because that's what you're doing - you're launching this person into a career in your company and in the MLM profession. You're also launching them onto the same emotional roller coaster that you've been on this entire time. Realizing that you have a responsibility to help prepare them for this is crucial.

Just like with the follow-up a quick and direct enrollment and launch is important. If possible, try to schedule your initial training/launching session with your new team member as close to when they joined as possible. Since I do a lot of long distance sponsoring I would conduct this over the phone.

The first thing I do is welcome them to the team and let them know how excited I am about working with them. Then I let them know that over the next 30 or so minutes I'm going to take them through a little orientation of our system and help them get their business started properly.

The orientation consists of me pointing out some of the resources available to them for support. We provide a team training website to our members and I point out where to find the getting started training as well as other important business building resources. Your leadership team has laid out for you support tools that are similar I'm sure and if they haven't then get in contact with your company to see what they provide.

Your team or company should provide some sort of getting started manual or step-by-step guide to help a new distributor navigate the process of getting their business set up. I don't sit there and walk the new team member through that guide, we provide videos that do that so they can go through it on their own (remember, we want to keep it simple). I then take some time and point out the corporate resources that will be important to them: their back office, their websites, product information, etc.

From here I simply take the new distributor back through the process they went through to enroll. I showed them how simple it was for me to make contact, pass their interest on to the system, send them to a 3rd party presentation, follow-up and get a decision. I ask them if they can see themselves doing that too? Then it's a matter of setting the new team member in motion. I suggest to them that they follow our training that calls for their first 24 hours of massive action. We encourage new distributors to make contact with a certain amount of people in their first 24 hours and invite those people to our presentation. I make sure they're clear on the process and then schedule a follow-up call with them for the next day. My purpose for the call with them the next day is to see how things are going. I want to see if they've been following the system and what reaction they're getting from their contacts.

> *"What we do for ourselves dies with us. What we do for others and the world remains & is immortal."*
>
> *-Unknown Author*

If they've been following the system they should be moving through a large number of people fairly quickly with very little negativity or time wasted. If that's the case then I encourage them to keep it up. If they express to me that they've been running into objections and skepticism then it's likely they are deviating from the system and they're taking too many people into the Valley Of Death.

Your responsibility as their "sponsor" is to coach them through this process. Remember my story with my friend Dylan? Remember how my excitement level dropped from a 10 to 4 after the first person I talked to?

Well the company I was in had a great training system but I didn't follow it. Unfortunately there are a lot of distributors in every company that feel the need to do their own thing. Because of this they often struggle more than they need to. But you can help save their MLM lives by keeping in close contact with them over their first week in their business - coaching them through the normal challenges they will face.

Enrolling a new team member isn't just a one-time event - it's an ongoing process of coaching, mentoring and relationship building. Yes, it's difficult to do this with every person you enroll. Sometimes you want to just let them find their own way but I promise you, the more people you launch properly the more duplication you'll see in your team.

However, there is a word of caution I want to throw out at you. There will be times when you have a distributor that appears to be going through the motions of building their business but they really aren't putting everything they have into it. They will call you and whine about the fact that they're doing exactly what the training says and they just aren't getting any results. Whenever I hear that I can see the hypothetical lie detector sirens going off. In reality that distributor really isn't excited about building a business and they were just looking for a lottery ticket - something they could join, do nothing with and instantly make a fortune.

The danger is to want success more for your new team member more than they want it for themselves. This is why we don't sell people into MLM. If we do then we're going to have to sell them to build and folks that is without a doubt the most frustrating thing to attempt to do.

I always tell people that I work with that my commitment to them is going to be a 100% reflection of their commitment to their business. That means if they do the work to pique the interest of 1,000 people and they want me to do 1,000 3-way calls with them I will. But if they do the work to pique the interest of 5 people and put me on the phone with just those 5 - then I will - and that's me supporting their business 100%.

Have you ever heard the saying, "You can lead a horse to water but you can't make it drink?" Well that is very true in our profession. All you can do as a sponsor is provide training and guidance. You can't provide the motivation to build. You inspire and lead by example but at the end of the day your distributor has to find his or her own pain. They have to be willing to go through their own ride on the MLM Emotional Roller Coaster!

6 YOUR RIDE BEGINS

So you are now riding on the MLM Roller Coaster. By now you've most likely experienced your first exhilarating dive straight down with your excitement level. If you have and you're reading this then congratulations, you've done a great job to stick with it. Believe it or not but 95% of Network Marketers quit at this point. They've talked to two or three of the people they were sure would join and when they do not, they quit. The goal is to stay on the ride for as long as you can - until you achieve your goals. Doing this requires many things that we're outlining in this book but what can help you and more importantly your future team members is being prepared for what they're about to encounter on this ride.

What I'm referring to are the many stumbling blocks or as Mark Yarnell in his book "Your First Year in Network Marketing" calls them, "landmines." These are challenges and obstacles that are going to cause your excitement level to dip as you build your business. The trick is knowing how to deal with them when they explode in your face and attempt to blast you right off the ride.

The first step is to understand that it's okay to experience adversity in your business. Unfortunately from the time we're little we're taught to avoid pain, challenges and difficult situations. We're always taught to play it safe and take the path of least resistance. The result of this is what you see in the economy today: 95% of the population working extremely hard while the minority 5% control 95% of the wealth. The wealthy people have learned to take risks and to invest in themselves while the average person is playing it safe.

If you take the time to study successful people you'll find story after story of people that have experienced massive struggles and adversity on their way to achieving success. One of my favorite books of all time is "Failing Forward" by John C. Maxwell. In this book Mr. Maxwell profiles people such as Amelia Earhart, Sergio Zyman, Tony Gwynn, Thomas Edison, Rudy Daniel "Rudy" Ruettiger, and many others. Each story gives further evidence that adversity is part of the path to success.

One of my favorite quotes of all time is from famous college football coach and icon Mr. Lou Holtz. He said, "Show me someone who is successful and I'll show you someone who has experienced massive adversity."

Everything you do in life can come with challenges. What determines whether you are successful or not in the things you depends on whether or not you seem them through. The mistake most new Network Marketers make is to assume that our profession would be any different than other professions because it isn't. So step number one is to recognize that experiencing challenges and setbacks in your business is just part of the process of becoming successful in this profession.

> "Show me someone who is successful and I'll show you someone who has experienced massive adversity."
>
> -Lou Holtz

And what kind of setbacks can you expect? Well let's start with one that we've mentioned briefly in an earlier chapter and that is the problem of improper expectations. When most new distributors start they are so excited that they just can't see why someone would not join their business. They make their list 100 names strong and begin the process of making contact with these people. What inevitably happens? That's right they take the first few people straight into the Valley Of Death where there is no return and they're left with no new sign ups and an excitement level of a 2 or a 4 and they're ready to quit.

The best thing you can do for yourself and your new team members is to help them understand that we don't need everyone to buy our product or join our team in order to have success. Show them the billions of dollars being generated by the industry you're a part of and help them see the numbers that are achievable with just a small sliver of that volume. People don't like to hear "it's a numbers game" anymore but it is still very true. There are so many people out there to talk to that we could spend our entire lives talking to people and we wouldn't come close to reaching everyone.

Another popular setback also comes in the beginning stages of reaching out to our contacts and that's the negativity that can be cast upon us. You know what I'm referring to. Grumpy Uncle Bob that just can't see how "one of these things" could ever work. Or perhaps it's cynical Aunt Sue that says she "tried that and it never works."

Let's face it, receiving any kind of negativity isn't fun and that's a big reason why many new distributors avoid talking to people, because they're afraid of the pain that might be caused from that negativity. The problem is that if we avoid talking to people how on earth can we build our business? So obviously we have to overcome this. One bit of advice I received early on in my career in this profession probably saved my MLM life and that was, "Don't ever take advice from people you don't want to be like financially."

If you take a step back and think about this for a moment it makes perfect sense. It sure did for me. I had some family members that I shared my business opportunity with that were downright nasty to me. They weren't just negative, they were mean. One actually threatened me physically if they found out that I was sharing my business with any of their friends. Now, most of that negativity came from ignorance about the MLM profession. You have to understand that people are naturally negative about something they don't truly understand. I look at it as a defense mechanism. If they're not familiar with it then it must be a scam, right?

Well I didn't let it affect me because I looked at these people and asked myself, "Do I want to be like this person? Do they have the lifestyle I desire?" The answer was, "No, they did not." So I didn't listen to them. I simply moved on and focused on finding the people for whom my opportunity was right for.

If the people you're talking to are casting negativity your way I want you to ask yourself if those people are the kind of people you want to be like? Do those people have the lifestyle and income you desire? Do they have the time freedom you're seeking? If not, why on earth would you let their opinion stop you from achieving your goals?

Continuing to push on through the negativity is key. And as you do so you're going to run into another familiar obstacle and that's what I call "the pretenders." They come in two forms. First they are the people you talk to that say they're interested, promise to attend the presentation or look at the DVD but they don't follow through. In reality they aren't interested at all, they're just pretending they are because it's easier for them to do that and then avoid you than to simply say they aren't interested.

The other form pretenders come in is as a new team member. They join your team, they're excited and tell you all the great things they plan on doing with the business. That obviously leads you to get excited and then magically those people disappear. It's almost as if they vanished into thin air. They don't return your calls or emails. They cut off their product order. They aren't getting on the company calls or webinars. They surely aren't attending any of live local events. They were a pretend builder.

When people join our team everyone is excited and everyone says they're going to do this or they're going to do that. Unfortunately the pretenders don't have a sign around their neck saying, "Ha-ha I'm just lying to you, I'm not really serious about changing my life, I'm just going to test it out and pretend to be in the business." Boy, if they had that sign it sure would be a lot easier to weed people out wouldn't it? But as I said, they don't have that so we're presented with an obstacle we have to get over.

Pretenders are difficult to deal with because they affect our emotions. They can seem so interested and just as excited as we are at one moment and then turn into a ghost the next moment, never to be heard from again. This can have a huge impact on our excitement level and it's another major cause of attrition in this industry. So how do you deal with this and get past the emotional scaring. Actually it's very similar to the way we deal with the negativity that gets thrown our way. I look at people who don't take advantage of my opportunity with pity. I say, "Shame on them for not taking advantage of such an incredible opportunity and missing out on the support I would have given them."

So far these have been some of the easier challenges to overcome. I know, you're thinking to yourself, "Are you crazy, these are major issues." And you're right, they can be a major hurdle to get over in your business. However, I don't think these are the biggest causes of attrition in our industry. What I feel is the biggest cause of attrition is when new distributors run into issues with their company or their product.

Let's face it; if you don't believe 100% in your opportunity then it makes it a little hard to be excited about sharing it with others. The problem is that there are no perfect companies or products out there and new distributors just don't understand this.

Earlier I mentioned the term "MLM Junkie?" This describes the Network Marketer that will join multiple MLM companies in a short period of time. In the years I've been a part of this profession the most companies I've ever seen someone join in one year was eleven. That's right, eleven companies in one year! The unfortunate thing here is that when you look back at all of those 11 companies most of them are very good companies, with leaders making great incomes in them.

So why would this person jump from company to company? Well, what likely happened is they jumped into the company because a friend of theirs was extremely excited about a new opportunity. They tried the product, liked it and then got started as a distributor. Up until this point everything was fine. Then, as that new distributor begins to build they run into a shipping issue. Maybe the company took 7 days instead of the 3 to 5 that was promised to deliver the product. Maybe the new distributor had to call into Distributor Support and was on hold for 10 minutes and got frustrated.

It could be a number of challenges that cause a new distributor to begin to lose belief in the company. Unfortunately for that new distributor they think it's up to the company to provide the motivation and drive to build the MLM business. It is not up to the company. The motivation to succeed in this profession must come from within you. Do you remember earlier we talked about "finding your pain?" Well, this is where having a good idea of what's pushing you to do this comes in handy.

What you must understand is that there are no perfect companies. It doesn't matter how successful a company is there will always be challenges. I was part of a company from 1997 until 2003 that was a $1.4 billion dollar telecommunications MLM company. They had over 2,000 employees and were the 4th largest long distance company in the United States. I joined the company right after they reached $1 billion dollars and they were in their 8th year in business. This company had all sorts of issues. There were customers getting billed improperly, poor customer service, etc. Yet this company managed to reach a level of success that most MLM companies will never reach.

How on earth did they do it? Well, for starters they had a group of leaders that believed in the product. It worked well, saved people money and they loved the idea of being able to make money from it. That was enough for them and they were willing to overlook some of the challenges that went on because of their belief. But these people also had internal motivations that were driving them to build their business even with they didn't want to. Even when distributors on their team would quit because they didn't want to deal with those issues, the leaders pushed on.

In my current company I'm involved in there were some initial challenges when we launched. There were a lot of people that joined in the pre-launch but when it launched there were a few challenges and some people left. Those same people who said this wouldn't work are now working in their 5th and 6th company since leaving our company.

What helped me push through those early challenges? Well, for one, I had the benefit of having a different perspective than some of those people who quit. I had been a part of a bigger company that had been around longer that had many worse challenges. That experience helped me understand that if that company could reach $1 billion dollars in revenue and create millionaires with the issues they experienced, then we were going to be able to ten times that.

In other words, I put the challenges into perspective. A new distributor feels that everything in their business has to be perfect in order for people to succeed. This comes from the fact that most people don't have the mindset of a business owner, they think like an employee. Employees don't have to deal with the challenges of running a business. They just show up for work, put their time in and then go home at the end of the day. The business owner is the one who has to deal with the payroll, the insurance, the lease, the medical, etc. They are the ones that have their business on their mind 24/7.

I knew that challenges were part of every business and that if the product was good and the company was committed to doing their part then there was no reason we couldn't be successful. I had a strong passion pushing me to build and I believed in the opportunity. That's all it took for me to be successful. Unfortunately most distributors lack the passion or the pain to build so all that's left is belief in the company and when something causes that belief to waiver then they're gone.

The result is they join a new company and for the first few months things are great. They think to themselves, "finally a business I can get excited about." Then the same old challenges present themselves and then they're off to the next company. Before they know it they've been in 5 or 6 companies in the last 12 months and what's worse is by now they've killed all the credibility they have with the people they know.

> *"Determine that the thing can and shall be done, and then we shall find the way."*
>
> *-Abraham Lincoln*

I mean think about it. If you come back to your personal contacts every few months with a new opportunity sooner or later you're going to have some people who start to see your MLM career as a joke. This is one of those things that give our profession a bad reputation. If people could just remember why they joined their company in the first place, focus on that, get excited about that, and then find their inner pain that pushes them to get past the normal challenges of building a business in MLM, then they could achieve tremendous results.

I feel another key to being successful in MLM is consistently working your business over a sustained period of time. In other words, working hard and not quitting. How can you build a long-term income with MLM when you aren't in a company for a long-term period of time?

Now, telling people to overlook some of the day-to-day challenges of their opportunity is a lot easier said than done. I completely understand how important it is that things go smoothly. But I also understand that it's impossible for things to always go the way you want. One piece of advice I can offer you (and one I hope you pass on to your team) is to look at your challenges and ask yourself, "In the big picture is this really that big of a deal?" I mean ask yourself, "Are there people in our company that are able to build successfully, despite these challenges?" If there are then perhaps what you're experiencing can be overcome.

I love it when people call me and proceed to tell me, "If we had ...then we really would be successful." Or they'll call to complain about something and say, "You know Ben, if such and such were different I could really succeed in this." What they fail to realize is that they're talking to a person that has been extremely successful in the company they're talking about. They also forget that I was here before they were and was able to succeed when the opportunity first started - when everything wasn't as good as it is now.

What you might need to do is seek out some assistance from your leadership team. Get on the phone with them and ask them how to deal with those challenges - because they've been through it. Now, I'm not saying you pick up the phone and complain to your upline. Remember, they're in the same company too and they know exactly what the issues are, trust me. Instead, pick up the phone and be a professional - be a business owner and offer a potential solution to those challenges.

Let me ask you, if you invested $300,000 to start a franchise and you started to experience some challenges would you close your store? Of course you wouldn't! What would you do? Well, you'd probably try to find solutions to help fix those problems. You'd probably contact the company you bought the franchise from and communicate with them on how to overcome those issues. In other words, you'd find a way to push through it and work it out.

In MLM we don't have to invest a lot of money to join so sometimes people don't have enough skin in the game and it becomes much easier for them to quit than to push through. Well, I have a simple way to keep you on the MLM Roller Coaster as you experience some of the dips and valleys of your belief level. When you find yourself losing belief in your opportunity and you feel like leaving the company remind yourself that you're not only quitting the company but you're quitting on your dreams too!

Wow, that's pretty strong language isn't it? You bet it is and it's 100% true. Now, I do understand that there will be some situations that can't just be overlooked and chalked up to a minor issue. If your company has major issues such as not paying you or your team or there are major ethics and integrity issues with the company ownership then that might be reason for you to rethink your situation. That was the case for me. In 2003 I made a decision to leave the only MLM company I had been with in my career. I joined them in 1997 and gave my life to that company. However, I saw some major issues with integrity at the top of the company that I felt was hurting my team, so I made a decision to leave. I was blasted by people I thought were my friends who said I was just "a hater" and "a quitter." I was called other names too. Sadly (yes sadly) that company dissolved their MLM division a year later and many of those same people who refused to see what I saw paid dearly because of it.

So yes, I understand that there may be times when a decision to leave must be seriously considered. However, if your company has good ownership that have a passion for MLM, has a good product and they do what they say they're going to do then there is no reason you can't be successful there. You obviously saw something in that company that you liked - or you wouldn't have joined. Focus on that and then find your pain that's going to push you to keep building - even when other people quit. That's the secret to staying on the ride!

7 IT'S DECISION TIME

If you've made it this far on the ride then you've had some ups and downs. You've felt the excitement of starting your new venture and you've experienced some of the initial challenges that go along with it. Now comes the hard part. Now comes the time when you have to make a decision. Are you going to treat this business like a hobby like the other 95% or are you going to take this business seriously and achieve your financial dreams?

If you have decided to kick your business into gear then it's time to go all in. Earlier I talked about "selling out" to your business. It is go time now. Either you get off the ride or you see it through. You can't build a successful business when you haven't completely given yourself to it.

Yes, you may be making phone calls consistently. You might be attending the live calls, webinars and local meetings. The next step is to "go core." You should already be a product of the product. You should already be talking to the people you know. Now it's time for you to attend your first major national event for your company.

The nightly calls, webinars and hotel meetings can recruit a team but it's the major national events that build a team and bond it together. Yes, the large national events can help with belief, in fact they are critical to developing more belief in your opportunity, but that's that what these events are for. These events are the glue that holds your organization and company together. They are where relationships are developed, ideas and experiences are shared and they are where the fun happens!

The major events open your mind to the big picture. In the world of technology it's very easy to fall into the comfort of working a home business. You get on all the calls and webinars and you feel like you're connected but it's very hard to connect with the passion and excitement of your company via technology. Network Marketing has always been a person-to-person business and the national events take that concept to a whole other level.

The first major national event I ever attended was in 1997, my first year in Network Marketing. I was 19 years old, didn't have a single person in my organization and I'd spent way more than I should have to attend. I slept on the floor of some cross-line friends I'd made in the company (because my upline was dead) and I survived for 3 days basically on breakfast bars. Looking at it from a practical standpoint, attending that conference wasn't a very smart financial decision. However, what I didn't know then was that it changed my life.

When I walked into that arena and saw 25,000 screaming, motivated, driven entrepreneurs something happened inside me. I was hooked on Network Marketing on a new level than I ever had been before - on a subconscious level. I remember coming home from that conference feeling like I was invincible. I truly let the company and opportunity get inside of me. That had a tremendous impact on my belief level that made talking to people much easier and of course had a positive impact on my business.

The motivation and belief you gain by attending these national events are important. But what I've learned is that the real benefit is what comes in between all of the general sessions and corporate trainings. It's the little things like getting to sit and laugh with your team. Hearing the stories of what the leaders went through to achieve their goals. This is where the relationships happen and that is glue that holds the organization together.

The best thing you could do for your team is to get them to the event with you and get them plugged into the leaders of your team on a personal level. If you don't have any team members then go out of your way to attach yourself to your leadership group at these events as much as possible. Even if it's just eavesdropping in the lounge in the hotel.

When I attend events with my team I will usually take a group of 20 or 30 people out to dinner or lunch. It's a tremendous bonding opportunity. Sometimes the people on your team will think you're untouchable because of a title you have or an income level you reach. Doing things like this will help remind them that you're human and you're just like them. Sharing the stories of your early days and what you went through will help to reinforce that they're on the right track.

Even if you only have 1 or 2 other team members with you, the impact is tremendous. Connecting on a personal level with your team members is what binds them together. The ups and downs of the emotional roller coaster will take its toll and the stronger the bond you have with those team members then the harder it will be for them to quit.

Yes, I know attending events is an expensive endeavor for some. From the cost of the flight, 2 or 3 days in a hotel, food, the conference cost, etc., you're looking at over $1,000. For some that might seem impossible. As I mentioned earlier, I was in that situation myself so I know exactly where people are coming from. However, this really is non-negotiable. The best thing you could do for yourself or someone on your team is to attend these national events.

Instead of looking at them as a "cost" look at them as an "investment" much the same way you would look at educating yourself. Some would argue that going to college is a cost while others would call it an investment into your future. I think evidence shows us that it truly is an investment. People that attend college statistically have a greater income and lifestyle over those that don't. Well, the same is true in Network Marketing. Those that invest in their personal growth and development have a statistically greater overall success in their business.

Attending your company's national events is the best possible investment in personal growth you could imagine and it's vital to your success and your team's success to attend them.

Now, just saying that to your team and expecting them to attend is not enough. This is especially true for the newer team members. They might say, "Well, I've already invested a lot to start and I'm excited enough, I don't really need to go, I'll go next year." If you think this way or you have team members that have said this to you then you have a hurdle that you must overcome.

This is when you must be non-negotiable with them! You have to make it clear to them that by not attending these events they are potentially sabotaging their MLM career. Waiting until the next one sounds reasonable at first but when you look at the statistics of our profession you'll see that the first 3 to 6 months of a new distributors business are the most critical. It is the time frame that most quit. Attending the national events will dramatically increase the odds of them sticking and staying.

8 BACK ON THE RIDE

By now you've returned home from your national convention with your company and most likely your excitement level is back to a 10. You feel rejuvenated, passionate about your product and opportunity, and now your posture is at a level that will begin to make recruiting easier. Let's face it, people want to be around other motivated and driven people. If you're happy and excited people will be attracted to you. You feel like you're walking on air and nothing can stop you.

Hopefully you've used this newfound passion to accelerate your growth of your team. Maybe you've reached your next promotion level in your business. Perhaps you've earned your first four-figure check. You say to yourself, "Yes! Finally I've made it!"

Then you wake up one morning, check your back office report and find that 60% of your volume is gone and with it 60% of your check. Your stomach turns and you feel like someone has just stabbed you in the gut with a knife. Perhaps a little panic even starts to set in. Your excitement level that was at a 10 has now dropped back down to a 4.

What has happened? Honestly, it could have been a number of things. Maybe your strongest leader decided to join another company. Maybe the company made a change with the compensation plan that drove some people away. Perhaps there was a problem with the product that wasn't communicated properly by the company and/or leaders. Possibly people just stopped building because they got burnt out. There could be a million reasons why people quit, leave, drop out, turn off product orders, etc.

Whatever the reason, this is a point where you will have an opportunity to experience another defining moment of your business. This is time in your business where you might question whether or not it's worth it to push through or just give up and quit. One of my mentors called this "Letting the tail wag the dog."

When you let the inactivity, negativity, or anything else of your team affect your business then that is letting the tail wag the dog. This is a very common occurrence in Network Marketing. It's very easy to get caught up in the challenges and negativity of your team, after all, you're bonded with them and what affects them affects you as well.

So how do you get past this point? The answer is to stay in what I call "Phase 1" of building your business. There are basically 4 phases you can fall into while building a MLM business:

- Phase 1 is actively recruiting new team members and gathering personal customers.
- Phase 2 happens when you begin to manage your small team that you've built.
- Phase 3 happens when the people that you had recruited begin to see you managing them so instead of building they start to manage their team and you begin to oversee their managing of their team.
- Phase 4 happens when your team sees you overseeing them so they start to oversee their team.

The ultimate result of phase 4 is negative momentum. You have more people doing nothing and dropping out than new team members coming in. Wouldn't you love it if everyone on your team were constantly in phase 1 of building his or her business? Of course you would! Well how can they get there if you aren't in phase 1?

Have you ever heard the saying, "People do what you do?" Unfortunately that's not true at all. If that were true, then everyone would be successful because every company has successful leaders to follow, right? The reality is that only people who are ready to follow your lead will actually follow it. The challenge is that if they have nothing to follow then the growth dies and along with it the momentum.

This is where the starting and stopping comes from in Network Marketing. You start building a team, get a little growth, then you begin to manage your team (phase 2). You start calling people on your team and asking them "why aren't you bringing people to the meeting?" You start looking at your report and asking people "why aren't you on $XXX amount of auto-ship?" Inevitably the people that you had brought on see you managing them and they have nothing positive to model so growth stalls - you get into phase 3 and 4. Then after everyone on your team has dropped off the face of the earth you start all over again.

The absolute best thing you can do for the growth of your team is for YOU to constantly stay in phase 1 of building your business. That way, when some of your team members finally decide to follow your lead, they will have something positive to follow.

The hard part is that it might take longer than you want for someone like this to present themselves in your organization. For most people, the smaller the team you have the more it feels like you're the only person doing anything. The worst thing you can do is start to look at your downline reports and ask "why?" In fact - don't even worry about looking at your downline report for your first year in your business. The only thing you should be focused on in your back office is your promotion tracking. You need to know what qualifications you need to meet in order to reach your next promotion level. You should never look at your reports and question why someone on your team is or isn't doing anything.

You might have heard the saying, "The speed of the leader determines the pace of the pack." By you focusing on modeling the proper behavior of actively building you will have team members that step up and decide to follow you.

9 PASSIVE INCOME

At this point your excitement level is hovering about a 7 but something soon happens that causes it to shoot right back to a 10. Your first leader pops on your team. All of a sudden you have someone that begins to enroll other distributors without your help. They might even be hosting their own meetings. You've just experienced your first taste of leverage and boy does it taste good.

For the first time in your life you're receiving income for something you didn't do. You're generating income from other people's efforts and you love every minute it. You think to yourself, "Yes! I've finally made it!" This is the time where many people take a little break or vacation or go on a little spending spree - after all they deserve it after all the hard work they went through to create this leader, right? Wrong!

This is another defining moment in your business. When your first leader develops in your organization there's something very dangerous that can set in and it's called complacency. This basically means you deluded yourself into thinking that you're done and now your leader is going to make you rich. This mindset is extremely hazardous to the success of your business.

When things begin to pick up this is the best time to step up your game even more. Instead of taking the extra money you're earning from your leaders growth and spending it on frivolous items - invest it into growing your team even more.

You should do more presentations and trainings than ever before. You should offer support to new team members in your organization - more than you ever have before. Now is the time for you to work harder than you ever have before.

I know, you're thinking, "But Ben, I've already worked hard, I deserve a break. I want to bask in the rays of financial leverage for a little while."

Unfortunately this mentality will kill your business!

Why? Well for starters, do you remember what I mentioned earlier about one of the keys to sustaining long-term success in your business? It was called staying in "phase 1" or continuous personal recruiting. Complacency will take you right out of phase 1 and stick you right into phase 2 and 3 - management mode.

Trust me, I know it feels great to have people joining your team that you didn't recruit. You feel like you can just now become a trainer to your team and be the "leader" that you think they need in order to guide them to success. Well, the leader they need is one that is a mentor, not a teacher. A mentor shows

> *"Success breeds complacency. Complacency breeds failure. Only the paranoid survive."*
>
> *-Andy Grove*

the way by modeling the proper behavior of success in our business. A teacher can inspire but a mentor is what people want to follow. Becoming complacent and falling into management mode isn't giving your team the proper behavior to follow.

The second thing you have to realize is that you really have no control of what people do or don't do on your team. Your loyal leader that you thought would always be in your team may decide to go to another company at some point. Or, perhaps they burn themselves out. They might even get sucked into the complacent mode of building their business.

If you've gotten away from phase 1 of building your business and you aren't adding new growth personally then when a leader drops out or their growth slows then so too does your check.

However, if you have been focused on adding new organic growth to your team then if one of your leaders begins to slow down, you now have new leaders emerging to make up for that loss of growth.

Now, this is easier said than done. There is a psychological hurdle to overcome here. It's very frustrating when one of your leaders loses their momentum. It's an emotional experience trust me! You can get so used to growth coming from a leg in your team and then when it's gone it hurts you emotionally, not just in your check.

You most likely have created a relationship with that leader too so that adds to blow as well. It's normal to feel similar to losing someone close to you or ending a personal relationship. But while this is an emotional business it's still a business and your mindset must look at it as one. Some leaders will fade away and leave to other companies. Others will slow down with their growth. Some just might not like you and what you teach your team and they just want to break away from you. Whatever the issue is you can't take it personally.

Yes, your excitement level drops! You're now back down to a 4 on the emotional MLM roller coaster. But, if you've stayed in phase 1 you have new growth to work with and a new leader is just around the corner.

The lesson in this chapter is a simple one: Don't put the success or failure of your business into the hands of any one leader on your team. Your mindset needs to be focusing on the fact that YOU create the success of your business and what a leader does or does not do in your organization is just part of the business.

The true long-term success in your business is not going to come from just one person or one leg. To create true success in the MLM profession (a six-figure income), you must have multiple legs of activity and you can't have that without building multiple legs.

So here's a logical question you might have at this point: When am I going to get to the point where I can stop working and enjoy that "walk-away residual income" that everyone talks about?

Unfortunately that's an impossible question to answer. There is no definite number or time when you can walk away. However, in the next chapter I'm going to show you how to create tremendous security in your business that will make creating long-term financial success a reality in your business!

10 DEPTH = SECURITY

When a new Network Marketer enters this profession they dream of the day when they will be able to wake up when they're done sleeping, walk on the beaches of the world while getting paid, and to travel to exotic locations 6 months out of the year. However, after the first 6 months of being involved in this profession those dreams can easily be dashed with the reality that this business is hard and it's going to take serious work to make it happen.

The good news is that it does work and you can have that dream lifestyle that most likely recruited you into Network Marketing. Unfortunately though, it's not as simple as sharing your product with people. It's not as simple as enrolling just 2 people and showing others how to do that too. It's not enough to talk to just one person per day for the next 3 to 5 years. To create the true walk-away income that you dream about it's going to take a lot of hard work and time. But hard work and time doing what?

Well, from earlier chapters you remember that as a beginner in MLM your focus should be almost entirely on personal recruiting - staying in phase 1 of building your business. However, as you begin to grow a team you'll be presented with an opportunity to accelerate the exponential growth in your business that leads to the massive residual income you desire.

You should always be leading by example and staying in phase 1 - always talking to new people, adding them to your contact database, and personal recruiting. Nothing mentors a team better than a leader that leads by personal example. But as you become more experienced you'll have a great opportunity to "pay it forward" - to assist your team members in growing their business too.

What I'm talking about here is building depth in your organization.

Depth is the key to creating the security in your team that will lead to true residual and walk-away income - income that allows you to walk on the beach for 6 months out of the year while you continue to get paid.

So how do you build depth? The answer is a simple concept but extremely challenging to execute. The answer is: teach others how to teach. To put it another way - your goal is to create leaders that replace you and your expertise. That's going to require you to build relationships, offer support and guidance, be a coach and mentor, and even act as a counselor and cheerleader at times.

This process begins the moment you enroll a new team member. When I sign up a new distributor I schedule what I call a "business launch" as close to when they join as possible (even the moment they join is fine too). This launch is where I do just that - help them to launch their business properly.

The business launch is where I walk them through the set-up of their business and our team's Fast Start Launch System. Your team or company most likely has a system for you to follow when new distributors join. I would recommend using that when you launch a new team member. This document or outline will help to ensure that the team member has a proper foundation to build their business upon.

During the first part of the launch session I'll cover some of the basics of where they can find some of their helpful websites, numbers/sites for support, etc. You need to make sure your new team member has the tools they'll need to build their business. They need to know how to order the product and where to enroll other distributors. Every company and team offers different tools and systems that they use to build. Find out what the most successful people in your company are using and follow that system.

For the most part the basic tools will be either a website or documentation that distributors use to present the product and/or business opportunity. This could be a DVD, a website, a brochure, etc.

If you're part of a product-based business then the distributor should have product on-hand that they can use as samples to give out to their personal contacts and people they meet. This is a great time to teach them the ins and outs of ordering product and the best way to do that is to help them place their first order.

Being part of some sort of communications system also might help. Most teams have an email or phone blast list to join. It's vital to get your team plugged into you and your upline so having a tool like this helps tremendously.

The next phase of the launch gets into identifying their "why." As I explained in an earlier chapter I call it "finding their pain." It's important for you to help them identify this and it's important for you both to write it down. Yes, I said both of you. Your new distributor is going to need a constant reminder of what that pain is. Remember, that's the motivation that's pushing them through the emotional MLM roller coaster!

You also need to write down their pain for two reasons. First, it's good to know what is important to the people you're working with. It helps you to connect with them on more of a personal level and that's always a good thing. Second, knowing what the pain is of the people you are working with means you'll be able to use that in your efforts of keeping them focused and on task (remember, one of your responsibilities as a leader is a coach and cheerleader at times).

Just like with you, there's going to come a time when your team member is going to experience some adversity. If you know their why/pain, you can help them make it through that adversity. I've used the pain of people I work with many times to help them fight through some of their low points on their emotional roller coaster. There will be times when people call me and say, "Ben, I need a kick in the butt."

That's when I pull out their why and hit them with it. For example, a gentleman on my team had a great motivating factor to build his business. He wanted to move his family out of the low-income housing he had his family in. He made a promise to them that he would do just that and the pain of letting them down was too much for him. That's what pushed him to build his business - even when he didn't want to.

So one day I get a call from this team member and he'd experienced some challenges in his organization. One of his key leaders had stopped building and he was letting that take him out of phase 1 of his business. That's when I turned around and reminded him of what his pain was. I also reminded him not to let the tail wag the dog and I helped him get refocused on where he was going. After that he was fine. Trust me, the more of the why's/pains of your team you know the better you'll be as a mentor and leader!

After you've identified their pain, now is the time to help them set their first short-term goal. Every company has a different compensation plan so whatever goal you're going to work with will likely have something to do with an initial part of the comp plan. For example, in our company we have a promotion that states when someone gathers their first 3 customers or enrolls their first 3 personal team members who are also customers of our product then they get something pretty special. The details of what they receive aren't important. The point I'm making is that we teach them to focus on getting their 3. That is the foundation to our comp plan. If they duplicate that small plan throughout their organization they'll have tremendous success.

Funny enough, we call this a "success unit." I'm sure other MLM companies call it something similar. Whatever you call it in your company you need to ensure that your new team member knows exactly what the requirements are to achieve it (what holes they need to fill in the compensation plan). Also make sure they know WHY they want to achieve this. Just telling someone to go do X, Y, or Z isn't going to be enough. If it's a boost in their bonus or commission level then explain that to them. If it's generating their first check then explain that. Be sure they can see what achieving that first goal is going to me to THEIR business.

Once they know where they're headed and what's pushing them to build their business (their pain) now comes the part of getting them to take action in their business.

> *"Teamwork. Coming together is a beginning. Keeping together is progress. Working together is success."*
>
> *-Henry Ford*

The first step is creating their contact list. This is without a doubt the most important part of launching your new team member successfully. Unfortunately it's also the most often overlooked step in this process. You can't just say, "Make a list of 100 names - use the memory jogger to do it." That's not enough. If you want to build a massive income in Network Marketing you have to be non-negotiable in this step.

Now, what I hear most often from a new team member is, "Well Ben, I don't know 100 people." Yes they do, they just aren't thinking big. When someone first sits down to create their list the only people that come into their mind are their friends and family and they might be thinking that they don't really want to work with some of their friends and family. The challenge is to get them to think beyond that.

You see some people may have friends and family that are driven, motivated entrepreneurs. My family however, was not that way and I would bet that most people's families aren't either. To help this new team member create an effective list you're going to help them first right down a list of as many people as they can think of - regardless of whether they feel they want to work with them or not - we'll sort that out shortly. Have them pull out their cell phone and scroll through the contacts. I've heard that the average cell phone user has over 200 contacts in their cell phone alone. Have them go through the contacts in their email address book. This is going to help spark their memory.

Yes, memory joggers help too. Most companies provide some sort of tool to help you remember people you know from your past and present. My goal is to help this person think of motivated, driven people that we can talk to immediately. So I'm going to have them try to identify people they do business with (store owners, real estate professionals, finance professionals, etc.). These talented people can add value to our team and I want to our business in front of those types of people immediately.

Now, what about everyone else? What about the average Joe or the family members on your list? Well, I truly believe you should make a list of everyone you know but that does NOT mean you should be "hitting" everyone you know with your opportunity. In our team we use a "checkmark" system. When we create a list of contacts we put a checkmark next to everyone that is a people-person, another next to someone that is money motivated (money is important to them), and another next to people that know a lot of people. Everyone that has 2 or 3 checkmarks are the ones we want to share our business opportunity with ASAP. The others we're going to politely share our product with.

Notice that I said "politely." There are too many Network Marketers giving our profession a bad name because they're out there trying to jam their product or service down everyone's throat. Listen, I know people can get excited about their product and that's wonderful. But some people go a little too far. For example, my son was invited to a classmate's birthday party a while back. Attending the party was another child and his parents came along too. These parents were decked out from literally head to toe in their company logo gear. I mean the mother had shoes that even said the company name on it. Then about half way into the party they start pulling out their samples of the product and they start forcing people to try it. Now, this wasn't their child's birthday party. Their child was invited to attend another child's party. Yet they continued to push their product on people and when someone refused to try a sample they gave a look on their face like the person who refused was delusional.

The entire time all the other parents are talking behind their back, "oh look, that's how those crazy MLMers build their business, I just could never see myself doing that." Sometimes with our passion and excitement we can offend other people and in the process end up hurting our profession and we don't need to do that to build our businesses. There are plenty of people out there for everyone and if you have a good product then the rest will take care of itself.

We teach a little more of a passive approach. With social-networking your team members could politely post something on Facebook (not 10 posts per day). They could send out an email. They could even mention it in passing. What should they say? Simple, "Hey guys if anyone you know is looking to _____, then I have something that might be able to help them. I'd really appreciate any referrals you could send my way."

Notice how you can replace the "_____" with any product or service in Network Marketing. Whether it's "lose weight, get healthy, save money on services," it really doesn't matter. The reality is that we need our team members to feel comfortable about reaching out to their warm market and if they feel like they're going to have act like an aggressive idiot while trying to shove their product and opportunity down people's throats then the odds are good that they won't be very excited about first creating their list and second reaching out to the people on it.

Once the list is created your goal is to have them identify at least their top 10. These are the 10 people that they would really like to work with. It could be some of their closest friends or even business owners that they know and respect and would like to work with. You're looking for 10 people who like the idea of making more money, who are people-people and those that have big circles of influence. If they say they don't know anyone like that they're lying. Everyone knows people like this - it's just that they're afraid to talk to them. Help them overcome this by throwing their "pain" back in their face!

Now that you have the top 10 it's time to get those people exposed to the business opportunity. This is where many leaders fail their new team members by leaving it up to them to do this on their own. That is very dangerous! That's like asking a baby to cross the street in busy traffic by itself, probably not the smartest thing to do.

Your new team member is what I call "a newbie." They don't have the proper posture needed to be effective in recruiting yet, so you have to be that for them. You have to coach them on how to make the calls. Use whatever script your company or team suggests but you as the leader have to physically assist the new team member in making those initial calls.

I tell my new team members, "let's get on the phone with these people right now and get them exposed to our 24/7 recorded presentation." Yes, they're a little uncomfortable with this but if you want them to be successful (I'm not talking about you, I'm talking about them) then you must help them overcome this.

Your goal is to help them get on the phone and just pique the interest of those 10 people - not to present to them. You must coach them to not say too much but to say it with excitement and urgency. It's more about how they sound on the phone than exactly what they say at this point.

By doing this, you should get at least 5 or 6 people to agree to look at your presentation. The next step is crucial. Your new team member has set a time to follow-up with their contacts that are viewing the presentation. That is when you are going to come in. You have to be the 3rd party expert for your contact. DO NOT let them tell you that they don't need your help - because they do!

I've seen newbies send their contacts to a presentation and after the presentation the person was excited and really enjoyed what they viewed. Then the new distributor gets on the phone with them and starts blabbing for hours about the parts of the comp plan and intricacies about the product.

When your team member is reaching out to the people they know it's vital that you be available to help during the follow up. The only thing your distributor should be saying in the follow up is, "So Joe Prospect, after looking at this information does this sound interesting to you? Great, I'd love for you to meet one of my business partners..." Then they 3-way you in so you can be the person that gets hit with the questions and skepticism. Leaving your new team member alone to do the follow up will inevitably lead to that rep quitting. I see it time and time again and it can all be prevented if the sponsor will just get involved a little bit.

Yes, I know, we always want new distributors to be self motivated and driven like we are. "Why can't they pick up the phone and just do it on their own - that's what I did." I can't tell you the number of times I've said that to myself or had it stated to me but regardless of how difficult it is we must see this through. It's like being a parent to a child. If you don't provide guidance and boundaries for your children then they're left to find them on their own and that will never turn out good.

So let's assume that you've done your job and you've helped this new distributor make contact and follow-up with their first 10 to 15 prospects and they have 1 that decides to join. At this point you have successfully launched your new team member. You taught them about the system, helped them order product and you helped them enroll a new distributor. They are completely trained on what it takes to be successful in your company - but you aren't done yet!

Now that this new team member has enrolled his or her own distributor it's time for you to begin to create a leader in your business. This is done by you modeling the behavior of a leader. One aspect is that of personal recruiting - you continue to personally enroll. But at the same time you're now going to show your 1st level distributor how to coach and mentor by doing just that with your 2nd level distributor (his 1st team member on his 1st level).

I know it's confusing but just hang in there with me. Let's call your personally recruited team member "Rep A" and we'll call your 2nd level team member "Rep B." Rep A has just enrolled Rep B - with your help. Now Rep B needs to be trained. So who does it? That's right, YOU do! The same way you launched Rep A is how you will launch Rep B. But here's a little secret: To build true leadership in your business you need to have Rep A watching closely as you launch Rep B. This will teach Rep A how to launch new distributors of their own and teaching your team members how to be independent of you as quickly as possible is your #1 goal.

You will assist Rep B in launching their business. You'll walk them through their launch packet/system. Then you will help them reach out to their top 10 to 15 personal contacts - getting them exposing the business opportunity immediately. Your goal is to help that new distributor enroll his/her first team member in their first few days in their business. While you're doing this you continue to support Rep A in sponsoring new team members.

So how do you find the time for all of this - especially if you aren't full-time in your MLM company yet? What you'll need to do is work efficiently. By this I mean combining presentations and trainings into groups of people rather than in a one on one setting.

For example, when you begin to work with Rep B (the distributor on your 2nd level) and you have them inviting prospects to a presentation, you can also have Rep A continuing to invite new prospects to the same presentation. Whether you're doing the presentation or not doesn't matter. The key is that you're working efficiently.

Once Rep B enrolls their first team member (Rep C - your 3rd level distributor) you'll repeat this process. Now, Rep A, Rep B, and Rep C are all inviting prospects to the same presentation. Then when you enroll Rep D (Rep C's first team member - your 4th level distributor) you continue. You'll conduct a business launch with Rep D while Reps A, B, and C watch and learn from you.

At this point Rep A should be able to do their own launches of new team members. Rep B should also be close to that as well. They should start to break away from your personal attention and begin focusing on driving their own growth. All the while you continue driving depth in this leg. Help Rep D enroll Rep E. Help Rep E enroll Rep F. Help Rep F enroll Rep G, etc. You do this until you hit a point that I call "bedrock." This is a point at which the distributor you and your team have enrolled won't follow the system and won't let you work with them. If this happens go back up to their sponsor and work with them to find another rep that will work with you.

Theoretically, you could be driving this depth forever. There really is no reason to stop. Even if you have a compensation plan that only rewards to a few levels - don't ever stop driving depth. Why? Because depth creates security in a MLM organization.

Let me explain what I mean. Assume you have a pay plan that pays out 7 levels deep and let's say you've built a team that has distributors on 7 straight levels, one on top of the other. Now, the rep on the 1st level obviously has 6 levels underneath them, right? Therefore he/she feels pretty good about things. They most likely have some good volume and growth on their team. But what about the distributor on level 7? He/she has no other distributors or volume.

What you want to have happen is for that 7th level distributor to have a 7th level distributor (your 14th level) of their own. You want that 14th level distributor to have a 7th level distributor (your 21st level), etc. You want this to happen because the more depth team members have in their organizations then the more likely they are to stick with the business. That in turn creates security for your business and income!

The hardest part about building depth is the fact that you're at the mercy of other people. Meaning, you can't build depth with people that won't let you work with them. This is one of the most frustrating parts of MLM. All you want to do is help that person be successful, but they just won't follow the system. They won't make the list, they won't follow the script, they won't get people to the presentation, they won't let you help with follow-up. They insist on doing things on their own.

On the one hand that sounds great - someone you don't have to work with. Unfortunately, 99% of the time this means a new distributor is about to die on the vine. They might give it a shot on their own for a few months, maybe even a year. But eventually they'll fizzle out and you won't hear from them again.

This is why it's so important for you as the leader to be non-negotiable with your new team members. It all starts with you so when you sit down to launch that team member, as tempting as it might be to just let them go out on their own, don't! Remind them that they're brand new and as good as they might think they are - they can't do this alone.

From that point it's up to you to follow through with your leadership role. Be excited about getting your new team members launched properly. And why wouldn't you be? Do you realize that every new team member you enroll means you're getting access to a brand new pool of prospects and it isn't going to cost you anything to generate them?

That's right FREE leads to talk to and you have an instant "in" with them - your new team member. Don't you realize that every distributor you enroll has access to people that you don't know - their warm market. Their warm market is your cold market (people you don't know). Don't you think they know some pretty good quality people? Sure they do! Well, here is your chance to get into that market and explode your business.

Let's say that each new team member you enroll and each one they enroll brings 100 names to their initial launch. If you have 1 new team member that means you have 100 FREE prospects to help them work. What if you've worked down 10 levels and now have the ability to help 10 distributors go through 1,000 prospects? At a 10% success rate you just grew your team by 100 new distributors!

What if you had 10 leaders on your team doing the same thing - working their own depth and getting into the markets of their team members? That would be 10 leaders working with 10 levels of reps, who each bring 100 contacts to the their launches. At a 10% success rate that means you'd have 1,000 reps per month joining your team! Take a look at your comp plan and find out what that would mean in terms of income to you.

This is why we build depth and why we teach others to do it too. But be careful. You can't build depth until you develop the skills and abilities to lead effectively. A new distributor should be focused on sponsoring and learning. You need to get yourself into a position of leverage before you can worry about depth. New distributors should be plugging their team members into the upline and the team's system to help maximize their time and growth potential. Then, as your skills develop and your income allows, you can focus more on building depth as your primary source of new growth.

In the beginning you should be 95% focused on personal recruiting and 5% focused on depth. As your team grows that number will change to 80% personal recruiting and 20% focused on depth. Then as you grow more it will go to 50/50. Then 30/70. Eventually as you become a superstar in your company you'll be spending 5% on personal recruiting (that's right you never stop) and 95% on driving depth through the markets of your team members.

11 EMPOWER YOUR TEAM

As your team develops and you begin to take on a leadership role it's very tempting to fall victim to what I call the "Big Ego Syndrome." At first it feels wonderful to have people calling you at all hours of the day. It's exciting for you when your team wants to put you on 20 3-way phone calls each day. You feel needed and appreciated and there's nothing wrong with enjoying feeling like that.

Unfortunately, now comes the part where I tell you that being the end all for your team is actually the worst thing you can do, not just for yourself but for your team as well.

I know that you feel like you're helping your team by doing all the presentations, calls and trainings. You feel good about yourself because finally you are the "big dog" in front of the room. But if you desire the true lifestyle freedom that sold you into MLM then you're going to have to get over this. Your goal is to empower your team with the skills of leadership. By you constantly being the leader to your team and their team members how can they grow as leaders themselves?

I see it all the time in our profession. An up and coming leader has a little team starting to grow. Maybe they have a few hundred people in their organization and the leader is doing all the presentations and 3-way calls for the builders of their organization. When they enroll new distributors they go out of their way to minimize the hurdles of their new team members. They might help them order their product - maybe even pay for it. They might call Rep Support for the new distributor (so the new team member doesn't have to wait on hold). They might even take their list and start calling people for them.

Perhaps you're reading this and saying, "But Ben, all the things you mentioned above sound like great things to do for your team, it sounds like you're helping them." Unfortunately what looks like help and assistance is actually debilitating their potential. You're cutting the legs out from underneath your team. It's like you're riding the roller coaster for them, trying to protect them from the adversity of the ride, while they're standing and watching. How are they going to learn how to navigate their own emotional roller coaster if they aren't experiencing it first hand? More importantly, how are they going to be able to help their team members navigate the roller coaster if they haven't been through it too?

Create Leverage

Your #1 goal in MLM is to create leverage. You're trying to create a situation where your organization and income grows while you no longer have to be directly involved in building it. This cannot happen if you don't have leaders developing.

Compare this to raising a child. When my first child was born through his first 15 months of life my wife and tried to protect him from everything. When he first learned to walk, we literally would walk behind him with our arms out trying to protect him from falling. We would constantly tell him to be careful when he tried something new. Then something hit me. How on earth is he going to learn how to deal with the adversities of life if he never experiences any?

As a parent this is one of the hardest things to come to terms with. You're basically saying, "Yes, I'm going to let my child fail and experience adversity in their life." From a common sense perspective that doesn't sound rational. But real life has shown us that our children must experience adversity if they're to grow into well-rounded human beings.

"If your actions inspire others to dream more, learn more, do more and become more, you are a leader."

-John Quincy Adams

When I am coaching an up and coming leader I explain it this way: I tell them, "How can someone be a leader to others if they have not experienced the adversity and challenges that their team is going through?" This helps that leader to realize that it's okay for their team to run into the bumps in the road. It's okay for them to experience the ride of the emotional MLM roller coaster.

It's also important to teach new leaders how to deal with the challenges that come along with being a leader. With a large organization of independent distributors comes a large amount of adversity that's going to be experienced. If you're going to survive the MLM roller coaster as a leader then you have to be able and willing to coach people through their challenges - without letting it affect your enthusiasm and commitment to your business.

In an earlier chapter I referred to letting "the tail wag the dog." The complaints and frustrations by your team can take a serious toll on your enthusiasm if you let them - if you let the tail wag the dog. By understanding how to deal with your team's adversity you cannot only help them through it but you can help yourself as well.

Do you throw water or fuel on the fire?

The phone rings, you see that it's one of your more active builders. He's in a panic and proceeds to tell you that his #1 person on his team is quitting to join another MLM opportunity. Here comes another defining moment in your business. You have an opportunity to help this distributor move past this or you can make it worse. Do you throw water on this small fire or do you add to it by throwing more fuel on it?

Many people say, "I want to throw water on it and put the fire out." And that would be the correct thing to do. Unfortunately what most up and coming leaders do is throw more fire on it. The proper thing to do would be to coach that team member through the situation and explain to them that this is part of the business and that there are many more people to talk to. Perhaps you tell a story of when the same thing happened to you and you're so glad you pushed through it because that same person that left has now been in 11 different MLM companies in 3 years. You explain how fortunate you feel to not have let that person's lack of commitment to their dreams to affect yours.

The MLM profession is made up of human beings and we are very emotional beings. We tend to make decisions based on emotions and this will be one of the hardest aspects of our business. On the one hand, we want people to be emotional and passionate about their business. On the other hand, it can backfire on you and take you right out of the game.

Emotional people tend to react before thinking rationally. This can lead to situations being blown way out of proportion. One of the best things you can do as a leader is learn the power of conflict resolution with your team. This means that sometimes you have to act as a counselor and help people work through their conflict. They might have had a disagreement with one of their team members. They could have experienced a challenge with the product or company. There are many adversities your team will experience where you will have to coach them through.

I recall one specific incident where a new leader on our team was having some great momentum. Their team was growing steadily as was their check. They were getting promoted up the ranks. Everything was progressing perfectly. But of course as their team grew more challenges that began to come up. You know what they say, "the more animals in the barn, the more 'do-do' there is to deal with."

In this specific situation, one of this leader's team members had a challenge with the product. It didn't work they way they expected and because of this they decided to quit. But of course they didn't just go quietly into the night. Instead, they decided to pick up the phone and call their upline leader and proceed to tell them all the things that are wrong with our company - justifying why they're quitting on their dreams.

This was the first time my leader experienced attrition and negativity towards their business. To say he didn't handle it very well would be an understatement. He called to yell at me about all the things his team member had complained about. He went on and on for about 30 minutes about how he didn't think he could continue to build his business because of these issues.

It can be very difficult to put your own reactions and emotions in check while you help someone resolve their conflict. Believe me, I wanted to jump down this guy's throat. After all, he was telling me (a top earner) that this couldn't work? I wanted to rip into him. This would have been a natural thing for me to do - to defend my opportunity. But I didn't. Instead, I let him vent. Sometimes your team just needs someone to talk to and sometimes you just need to be there to listen.

After his little 30-minute rant I told him to take a step back and relax. I explained to him about the challenges of our business. I shared my past experiences where I had leaders quit and try to bring me down with them. I refocused him on what his "pain" was and helped him to regain his vision for his business.

It would have been very easy for him to quit, as that's what most Networkers do. When the negativity starts at the lower levels and works its way upline it can leave a wake of attrition in its path. But thankfully I took the time to help coach this leader through his conflict. I helped him resolve his concerns and open his eyes to the big picture. The best thing I helped him to see is that by him experiencing this he was earning his leadership wings. He could see that he could now help someone else through this same situation. A leader was born at that moment.

As you continue to ride the MLM Roller Coaster and your team begins to grow so does your responsibility to your team to push through the adversity of our profession. Yes, it would be a lot easier just to quit and walk away from it all. But the path to achieving your dreams is not easy, nor will it be for your team. Your biggest gift you can give to your team is leading by example and not giving up on your business.

12 LEVELING OUT YOUR EMOTIONS

At this point in your business you should notice that the distance between the highs and lows of your emotions should be getting closer. You are simply getting used to the ride. In other words, you're becoming a leader. If you've made it this far or are hoping to make it this far in your business then you can get excited because those that reach this point are usually headed toward long term success.

So many people in our incredible profession give up before they've even given themselves any chance to succeed. And as you've noticed emotions have a big role in that. Therefore getting your emotions to an even keel is a critical step towards achieving success in the MLM profession.

One of the best ways to do this is through self-development. Believe it or not but I think self development is the most important aspect to focus on in your MLM career.

The reality of our profession is that it's hard - just like anything that gives you the ability to achieve your dreams. My favorite quote of all time comes from Tom Hanks in the movie "A League of Their Own." In the movie Tom Hanks is talking with one of his female baseball players (played by Gina Davis). Her character has decided to leave the team just before the playoffs because "it just got too hard." Hanks' character replies, "It's supposed to be hard. The hard is what makes it great."

I agree 100%! I love the fact that this profession is difficult. It makes it so much more rewarding when you achieve success - because you know you've done something that other people wouldn't do. The key is giving yourself the tools to make it.

That's where self-development comes in. This is without a doubt one of the most important "crutches" that you'll need to lean on in your career. Think about it for a minute. Your mind controls your actions. Your action controls your results. If you have a weak mindset then you take weak actions and inevitably get weak results.

There are many forms of self-development and you could easily spend a small fortune on them, but I don't think you need to. There are so many amazing resources out there to benefit from.

One of the best sources you'll have is your successful leadership in your company (your upline). They've walked in your shoes and know exactly what it's going to take to succeed. Notice that I said "successful" leadership. Just because someone is "above you" in the genealogy doesn't instantly give them the right to lead you. Look for the people in your leadership line that have the lifestyle you desire and attach yourself to them.

I feel your leadership team in your upline is one of the best sources of self-development because these people have achieved success in your company. There are many generic trainers in our profession that certainly deserve respect and you can and will learn a lot from them. But if you're looking to be successful in your chosen company then it makes sense to be following the lead of people that have come before you in that company.

What you want to learn from these leaders is not just the nuts and bolts (those are important and you want to learn those too). You ultimately want to attach yourself to these leaders and learn from them on a consistent basis in all areas of the business. Your goal is to absorb as much information as you can about who that person is, what they've done to reach their levels of success, and how they've managed to make it through the ups and downs of their personal MLM Roller Coaster. Then, you want to model yourself after these people.

Modeling yourself after successful leaders is one of the best ways to speed up your personal and professional growth. You should constantly be learning from these successful leaders and be looking for ways to make yourself better. Model everything - how they talk, the jokes they tell in the presentation, the stories they share, the way they handle adversity, etc. Doing this will give you somewhat of a blueprint as to what you're striving to become as a leader in your company.

One of the best places to be able to model your successful leaders is at live company events. The major national events are perfect places for beginners to be able to sit back and observe their successful leadership in action. Yet another reason why attending live company events are so important!

Working on Your Mind

From here you're going to have to work very hard on growing your mind. I think it's vital to have a routine of self-development that you stick to. There are so many distractions in our life, some positive and many negative. You need to constantly be feeding your mind with positive, reinforcing information.

I recommend at least 60 minutes per day. I do 30 minutes in the morning (it's great to start your day with positive information) and 30 minutes before you go to sleep at night. Please note that this self-development time DOES NOT count toward time spent building your business!

Now, there are many forms of self-development. There are books, CD's, DVD's, MP3's, etc. I have two small children, a wife, I play in a men's baseball league, go to the gym 5 days per week, volunteer my time in my children's classrooms, help coach their different sport teams, etc. I'm pretty busy. Most of my reading time is reading children stories to my kids before bed. Therefore I have to get creative. This was especially true before I went full-time in MLM. When I was working a 50-hour a week job I was really pressed for time.

So what I did was change things up a bit in my routine. When I went to the gym I would listen to my MP3 player and it was filled with some extremely motivational music - the kind of music that would get me extremely pumped up. What I did was replace the music with self-development training. To this day I am constantly downloading audio books onto my MP3 player. I'm always looking for generic training from the MLM superstars in our profession and putting their information on my MP3 player as well. When I get in the car, instead of listening to satellite radio, I connect my MP3 player and I'm listening to the self-development material.

Any chance you can get to improve yourself is time well spent. I will say that if your schedule is extremely tight then you're most likely going to have to be making calls to prospects in those nooks and crannies of your day so you might have to sacrifice something else to make time for the self-development. But please, make the time for it. It's one of the best investments you'll ever make.

Here are just a few recommend books to start with:

"Developing the Leader Within You" - John C. Maxwell
"Failing Forward" - John C. Maxwell (can't go wrong with Mr. Maxwell)
"Think & Grow Rich" - Napoleon Hill
"The Greatest Networks in the World" - John Milton Fogg
"Tribes" - Seth Godin
"Beach Money" - Jordan Adler
"Making the First Circle Work" - Randy Gage
"GoPRO" – Eric Worre

13 STAKE YOUR CLAIM

At this point you're thinking, "Well, I've been through a lot but now I've got a solid team growing, I've been promoted a few times, I've made it." No you haven't! The moment you think you've arrived is when you begin to lose in this profession. Complacency is a major killer of momentum in MLM.

Yes, you can be proud of yourself for making it this far but now is not the time to slow down. In fact, now is the time to work even harder. I know you're thinking, "But Ben, do I ever get to stop? What about the dream of walking on the beach and making money, do I ever get to live that out?" The answer is absolutely yes, just not yet.

So when is yet? Well, it's different for everyone and every company's compensation plan but I will say that if you can get 15 to 20 leaders creating more income in their MLM business than they ever had with their regular J.O.B. then you've most likely reached a point of sustained momentum - where no matter what you do or don't do your business will grow without you.

Therefore, if you haven't reached this point you need to forge ahead. Now is the time for you to stake your claim as a future MLM Rock Star (thanks Randy Gage)! Now it's time for you to really dig in with your company. Get involved with the corporate leadership and make yourself known to them. Seek out hotspots in your team and offer support to help them explode their business. And above all turn your blinders on to the outside MLM world.

Surviving the MLM Emotional Roller Coaster means staying consistent with income producing activities over a sustained period of time. You will have good and bad distractions that will attempt to derail your ride. You will have people question your sanity. Your loved ones may even talk behind your back. It won't feel good. But if you're willing to endure these short-term challenges you'll find a level of success you didn't think was possible.

As you grow into this profession you have great responsibilities to yourself, your company and to our profession to represent yourself professionally, with character and integrity. The industry of Network Marketing/MLM is changing and if you choose to stake your claim as a leader you'll need to adapt and help others do the same.

I wish it were as easy as just going through the motions. I wish there was a MLM "easy button," but obviously there isn't. If you embrace the challenges and understand the bigger picture you'll see that anything can be overcome. If you approach each day with a passion to help others benefit from your opportunity and your products you'll see that your "job" not only becomes easier but also more fun.

This is what it means to stake your claim inside of MLM. To become an influential part of this community you need to embrace it, all of it, the good and the bad. You also need to commit to making it better. The best way I know how to do that is empowering others with the knowledge that I've gained through the years. You might call this "paying it forward."

Learning and mastering the skills of Network Marketing isn't enough. You need empower others with that mastery as well. This is the key to bringing it all together. Yes, if you help enough people become masters of this profession, you will have the success you desire.

Enjoy the ride!

ABOUT THE AUTHOR

Ben Sturtevant resides in Santa Rosa, California with his wife and two children. He became involved in Network Marketing/MLM in 1997 at the age of 19 while in college. After getting into a career in Physical Therapy, Ben realized that being his own boss and building passive income was where he wanted to go with his future.

Ben has created organizations of tens of thousands of distributors and customers and has earned millions of dollars in his career. He has been the #1 income earner in two companies and has also served as Chief Marketing Officer of a Network Marketing company.

Ben's passion is helping his team and fellow Network Marketers create success. He created the RealNetworker.com resource to give all Networkers access to training and support to help them build their businesses.

To learn more about Ben you can visit www.realnetworker.com.